RICOCHETS

RICOCHETS

From Gordonstoun to Africa's wars
The life of mercenary soldier Peter Duffy

GRAHAM LINSCOTT

ISBN 978-0-620-72217-9
eBook ISBN 978-0-620-72218-6

Adventure / Mercenary wars / Sky-jacking / Humour

Layout: Jo Marwick
Photographs courtesy of Independent Newspapers KZN

Published by Nomapix (Pty) Ltd
maclaines@imaginet.co.za

TABLE OF CONTENTS

FOREWORD

Peter Duffy is an eccentric adventurer with life experiences that include: coffee planting in Tanganyika; seriously practising karate in Japan; spells as a film stunt man; serving as a mercenary in the Congo; a hectic career as a press photographer; invading the Seychelles Islands with a mercenary force; hijacking an airliner to escape from the Seychelles; and several years in Pretoria Central Prison for the hijacking exploit.

Born into a well-to-do Scots family, he was educated at Gordonstoun (as were Prince Phillip and Charles, Prince of Wales) but soon left for the freedom and wide open spaces of Africa and all the mischief that beckoned.

Duffy has pursued his chequered career with high good humour and an infectious zest for life. He is a character writ large.

EARLY DAYS

"I cannae see the wee bairn. Lift him ontae the bench." An orderly lifted Peter Duffy onto the bench of the dock in the juvenile court in Elgin, Scotland. It satisfied the magistrate. "Ah, that's better. I can see yer noo." Duffy was all of four years old. He was in the dock along with his brothers Derek and Brian, five and four years older respectively, for a piece of larceny in the town. At the railway yard they had pulled back a tarpaulin to find a truck stacked with boxes of shiny ballbearings. These had fitted the pouch of the catapults each wore about his neck, as if designed for it. The ballbearings were possessed of an accuracy and velocity through the air that small boys could only dream of. Across the tracks stood an old goods shed, its windows opaque with the soot and grime of decades. It was an invitation not to be resisted. The Duffy boys discovered that the ballbearing ammunition practically sang as it smashed its way through the glass panes. But the long arm of the law had caught up with them, and here they were before the juvenile court, a disgrace to the family.

The brothers had spent the war years, also the immediate post-war years, at Elgin with their grandmother, Jessie and their grandfather, David Hughes, a prosperous chemist in the town who had been a sniper in the Black Watch during the First World War. Their mother, an attractive blonde divorcee named Marion was of the Scots gentry. She had spent the war in England. Peter never knew his father. Marion visited whenever she was able but the three ran wild in the small Morayshire market town (technically a city because of its ruined cathedral) and the surrounding countryside, running their grandmother ragged at times and giving their grandfather wry amusement.

At times the grandfather's forbearance could also be tested. He came home for lunch one day to notice his cabbages wilting and smoke wreathing its way out of the soil. Whatever could this mean? Investigating further, the soil suddenly gave way beneath him and he found himself in a fiery pit, engulfed by smoke. He might as well have been back on the Western Front. The boys had emulated the escape tunnels which were the theme of so many current war films. They dug it under the cabbage patch, shoring up the roof with a sheet of zinc. Then they gathered beech leaves to light a fire underground. And then they tested the efficacy of the gas masks with which every household had been issued during the war. The efficacy was not great and they had barely emerged spluttering when grandfather came home. The older boys took off like greyhounds. Peter climbed onto the roof of the house and it was nine o'clock at night before he could be persuaded to come down.

Derek and Brian went to the local primary school. Peter was eventually to go to Arbelour, preparatory school to Gordonstoun, Scotland's premier independent school, modelled on Germany's Schule Schloss Salem, which was in turn modelled on Eton. All three were to end up at Gordonstoun, which had been the school of today's Duke of Edinburgh and was also to be the school of Charles, Prince of Wales, and his brothers, Princes Andrew and Edward. The Duffy boys were socially out of the top drawer. Larceny in a railway yard was most certainly a deviation. But they escaped with a stern reprimand, the older boys receiving particular censure, and for all three of them life carried on much as it had before in Elgin.

One of the places they visited regularly, and with fascination, was the Elgin Museum. The Scots are great wanderers. They served as soldiers, explorers, missionaries and administrators in every part of Victoria's empire strung about the globe, and they brought back with them all kinds of mementoes of far-flung and exotic places. Many ended up in places such as the Elgin Museum. The Duffy boys, Peter in particular, looked at and (illicitly) handled with fascination shrunken heads from South America, barbed spears and poisoned arrowheads; daggers and swords, cowhide drums, fabrics and artwork of outlandish colour and design. These spoke of a world out there of heat, colour and passion; of a vibrancy that was quite absent from the highlands of post-war Scotland.

Then Marion remarried. Her new husband was Aubrey Sassoon, an Englishman who was a Lloyds underwriter in the City of London. The boys relocated to a London whose grimness and post-war austerity altogether escaped them. Here in Knightsbridge was a glittering world from beyond their ken. Their house was near the home of Group Captain Peter Townsend, so often photographed in the newspapers in the company of Princess Margaret. Several foreign embassies were in the vicinity and many a diplomatic grandee found himself smothered in the snow that inexplicably slipped off the Sassoon rooftop as he walked past on the pavement below.

To return to the Elgin juvenile court, it would be some five decades before Duffy found himself in a similar setting. This time it would be the Natal Supreme Court, sitting in Pietermaritzburg, capital of the South African province of Natal. With him in the dock were a former British army officer; several serving members of the South African army special forces; and a motley of mercenary soldiers from several continents. The charge: air piracy. They were alleged to have attempted a coup d'etat on the Indian Ocean islands of the Seychelles and to have hijacked an Air India passenger aircraft to make their escape when things went wrong.

Between these two points in Duffy's life lie: East Africa at the fag-end of empire; fighting with a mercenary force in the Congo; a stay in Japan to become skilled in karate; a career as a film stuntman, first in Japan then in Ireland; and a career as a newspaper photographer in South Africa. Then, subsequently, life (and survival) in Pretoria Central prison plus a picking up of the pieces after his release on parole.

For Duffy, life has not been dull. Those ballbearings have never stopped their sweet whistling.

GORDONSTOUN

Life at Gordonstoun was Spartan in the extreme. The day began, winter or summer, rain, snow or shine, with a pre-dawn run about the school grounds wearing nothing but a pair of shorts and tennis shoes. Located on what had been the 150-acre 17th century estate of Sir Robert Gordon, the school is close to the Cairngorms mountain range and to the North Sea. It would be difficult to imagine more extreme climatic conditions on mainland Britain. The morning run was followed by a cold shower, mitigated only slightly by a dashing of hot water from the handbasins by the boys onto their frozen bodies before diving under the icy jets of the showers. The proceedings were closely monitored by the colour bearers (equivalent of prefects) and the housemasters. Nobody escaped the run and the cold shower. It got the heart going, it made a man of you and it underpinned the ideal of education based on wholesome outdoor pursuits, first advocated in Germany by the Anglophile Kurt Hahn then transplanted to Scotland during the rise of Nazism. The cold run and the cold shower were followed by a cold breakfast, a muesli-style concoction of oats. Then the day began in earnest.

Mornings were devoted to the normal academic disciplines, afternoons to outdoor activities. Gordonstoun offered rugby, football, hockey and cricket, but there was also a strong emphasis on seamanship and sailing, cross-country running, obstacle courses, mountaineering and mountain rescue and mapping and orientation in the Cairngorms. The school ran its own firefighting unit, which was available for deployment anywhere in the district, as well as its own lifeboat service. Morayshire seemed the ideal locale for putting into practice the ideals of healthy outdoor activity, as expounded by Kurt Hahn. Cadet activities were also an important feature of school life, Britain's three services – Royal Navy, army and Royal Air Force – all of them represented and with a strong encouragement to boys to follow careers in the military.

The Gordonstoun boys had the simplest of uniforms. Blue-grey shorts almost down to the knee; grey open-necked shirts – no ties ever; blue-grey stockings; and blue-grey sweater when the school authorities deemed the temperature to have become frigid enough to justify it. The shorts had no side pockets, only a back pocket, which Gordonstounians maintain accounts for the habit of both Prince Philip and Prince Charles to hold their hands behind their back. For both of them, for several years the back pocket was all there was. The only time Gordonstoun boys wore long trousers was when they put on seafaring blues for seamanship classes at the nearby fishing port of Hopeman Harbour.

Discipline was strict – lights out early in the evening in the different houses and no tolerance of any kind of deviation. Yet there was an acceptance of the rules, an esprit de corps. The cane was a sanction kept very much in the background (unusual in British and Commonwealth schools of that era) and used only for the most egregious offences where there was no other remedy. Once Duffy was caught with several other boys, while still at Arbelour, the preparatory school, sliding on the ice of a frozen pond in a spot that was very definitely out of bounds. A master was seen coming through the woods with his dog and the boys ran for it. But one was still stranded on the ice and Duffy stayed with him with a long branch he had plucked from a tree to assist if anyone should fall through the ice, which could have had dire consequences. All the miscreants were eventually identified – they owned up – taken before the headmaster and caned; that is, all except Duffy. It turned out he was spared because he had chosen to stay and protect his school chum rather than run, which he could have done. The incident was at the prep school but it captures the Gordonstoun ethos of honesty coupled with resourcefulness, courage and loyalty. Duffy was never to forget it.

It was a harsh but healthy life at Gordonstoun. The brothers overlapped for a few years in their time at the school and were all three of them noted for their proficiency and athleticism on the obstacle courses. An eight-foot wall was a challenge not an insuperable obstacle. They had spent their early years clambering over such obstacles in the Morayshire countryside, often pursued by bailiffs and landowners, and it was second nature to them. They also took to seamanship, sailing and rowing the school's cutters with zest.

Deviation from the rigidity of Gordonstoun was difficult. One seized small opportunities as they presented themselves. One was in Scripture classes where Duffy gave early expression to what was to become a lifelong antipathy toward religion by, before the class began, inserting a sixpence to the electric light socket, between the terminals and the bulb. As the Scottish evening drew in fast, the master would pause in his droning from the Bible to switch on the light – and it would, of course, immediately fuse. The sabotage never was detected. Duffy would retrieve the sixpence before the electricians arrived to investigate and put in a new bulb.

But this was small recompense to a restless spirit. Was there no other way to buck the Gordonstoun rules, even if ever so slightly? Duffy hit upon it temporarily. The three-times weekly bicycle ride of about four miles to Hopeman Harbour for seamanship instruction was irksome. It was generally made in pouring rain and freezing weather, often in sleet and snow. Duffy and a group of chums discovered that, for a few shillings each between them, they could hire a taxi. Elgin had a stately taxi fleet of veteran Rolls Royces. They would order a taxi, meet it at a designated spot near the school then take a Rolls to Hopeman. They developed a regal wave for their fellow-Gordonstounians as they passed them on the road, pedalling through the rain. Of course, it could not last. This was absolutely counter to the rigorous ethos of the school. Somebody reported them. Duffy and his group were severely reprimanded and punished. Once again they pedalled between Gordonstoun and Hopeman.

Could there be anything more substantial in the way of bucking the system? Well, yes. The boys took their meals in a dining hall in the main Gordonstoun building. Serving up were maids employed in various capacities at the school and in the staff quarters. Among these was Jeanette Edgar, a striking sixteen-year-old whose fair hair and Nordic facial features matched the Scandinavian origins of her name. She was a housemaid in the headmaster's house and would come across every evening to assist at table in the dining hall. She was a stunner. Duffy caught her eye, human electricity jumped the gap and one thing led to another. Duffy was allowed to train for road-running on his own in the early evenings. In the gloaming he would meet Jeanette in her home village of Duffus, on the edge of the Gordonstoun estate, and they would repair to a nearby graveyard for carnal bliss in these ghostly surroundings. At other times he would take her on the bar of his bicycle to secluded spots in the woods. Best of all, when he was on coastguard duty at the lighthouse manned all year round by the Gordonstoun boys, he would slip away when his watch ended at night (the coastguards slept at the lighthouse) and take her to a nearby cave in the cliffs. The affair lasted a couple of years, until he left Gordonstoun and set sail for Africa, and it never did leak out. This surely was one of the better-rounded Gordonstoun experiences. Very much outdoors but probably not quite in the way Kurt Hahn had envisaged.

LONDON

Duffy left Gordonstoun in 1957, his best result being in geography, which fascinated him, opening up the wide world of open spaces, sunshine and vibrant cultures of the British overseas colonies – as they then still existed – which could hardly have contrasted more in his mind with a grey-toned Britain that was still clambering out of post-war austerity. The Swinging Sixties were still over the horizon. The sunshine and savannah of Africa beckoned. But how to get there? How to set oneself up? Duffy gradually went about it. But meanwhile he had to make a living and scrape together some savings. Not for him a career in one of the professions or in finance or business (in spite of his stepfather's connections in the City). His parents had moved away from London to Cornwall so he took a bedsit in Maida Vale and worked in a series of coffee shops, Jolyons corner shops and a fruit juice bar in Mayfair, a novelty in those days. He saved every shilling he could, made easier by the fact that in those days he was a strict teetotaller and did not smoke. He ate on the job and his wants were few. He saw everything as temporary, yet Jolyons sent him on a trainee manager's course. Behind the serving-up counter in his Jolyons waiter's outfit one lunch hour, he suddenly found himself looking into the face of a boy who had been with him at Gordonstoun. This individual was overcome with embarrassment and confusion. Gordonstoun boys went on to careers in the army, navy or air force; or at law or in medicine or in business and finance. They did not become waiters in Jolyons shops. But Duffy had his priorities elsewhere. He carefully ladled up the food each mealtime, judiciously relating the size of the portions to the size of the many female customers' breasts. They needed that bit extra to keep them going. He became very popular with some of his customers.

Then he received a financial leg-up when, through connections of his brothers, he found employment as a building site labourer, working for a partnership of two former public schoolboys who specialised in refurbishing rundown old buildings in the Earl's Court area. Work as a building site labourer is even further removed from the usual Gordonstoun career path than being a waiter in Jolyons, but the pay was considerably better. Duffy learned the tricks of the trade fast and picked up the Cockney argot. He knew he'd been accepted when one of his workmates, an Australian who had been in London for years and had himself become Cockneyfied, showed him, during a tea break, a newspaper report about two prisoners who had escaped from Dartmoor, in Devon, and were on the run. "Don't tell nobody," said his new chum, "But vem two, they's stayin' wiv me 'ere in 'Ackney. Good blokes!" As a salt of the earth working man, Duffy had arrived.

Then, through a friend of a friend, he heard of a position that had become available as a trainee farm manager in Tanganyika, the British protectorate – once a German colony – on the East Coast of Africa. Duffy had read of the coffee growing industry in Tanganyika and saw this as a worthwhile option. This position was on a mixed farm, not a coffee plantation, but at least it was in Africa and a step in the right direction. A lengthy correspondence ensued by sea mail with the farmer, who had the unlikely name (for the Irishman he was) of George Muvenheimer. At length it was agreed: Duffy would go to Tanganyika under his own steam to work on the Muvenheimer farm for a year, learn the ropes and learn how to speak Swahili.

In 1959 at the age of 19 he took a berth in the bowels of the small British India liner, Uganda, that plied between London, the East Coast of Africa and India. His mother and stepfather did not particularly support the venture – the colonies were simply beyond their ken – but did not argue when Duffy insisted. Besides his savings from working in London, Duffy had with him a cheque for £100 from Aubrey Sassoon, an advance of what he was due to receive on his 21st birthday.

The trip was uneventful until Gibraltar. Duffy admired from a distance a leggy and lovely first class passenger who was on her way to Kenya to marry her fiancée, a big game hunter. His admiration was from a distance because the young men in first class, not to mention the ship's officers, were all over this girl. Then, when they were just out of Gibraltar and heading eastward in the Mediterranean toward Port Said and Suez, Duffy was standing at the poolside deck bar when he spotted a small child in difficulties in the water. He dived straight in with his clothes on and rescued the child without any difficulty at all. Suddenly he was a hero, a celebrity. When he returned from changing his clothes, the child's parents and various other passengers were all over him. For the rest of the voyage he found it difficult to pay for a drink. And among the people suddenly making a fuss of him was this leggy young stunner. Duffy found himself in deep conversation with her, something he could not have aspired to before. One thing led to another.

One of the officers was also paying much attention to the girl and was highly suspicious of Duffy, openly hostile. Then one morning he caught Duffy in the first class section of the ship, where second and third classes were not allowed. He marched Duffy out and next morning a stern notice at the purser's office warned second and third class passengers against venturing into first class. It seemed Duffy was thwarted. First class passengers could go where they liked, but what girl could be tempted to a shared cabin just above the propeller shaft?

But the leggy girl had a corner cabin in the superstructure above the main deck, with a porthole looking out to the port side. Lashed to the deck beneath it was one of the ship's anchors. It was simplicity itself for Duffy to climb up the anchor every evening and go through the porthole for a night of dalliance with his new lady friend. It happened all the way down the Mediterranean, down the Suez Canal, down the Red Sea and into the Indian Ocean, right up until they reached Mombasa. One night, as they entered the Indian Ocean after Aden, a storm blew up. The crew went about closing all the portholes, including the one Duffy had just used. Then they went about the passenger decks, checking that doors were closed and everything was properly stowed to ride out a storm. A crewman opened the unlocked cabin door to discover Duffy and his lady love in flagrante delicto, riding out a different kind of storm. He left with tact and Duffy left again through the porthole, which he managed to open from the inside.

When they reached Mombasa they parted company, never to meet again. A shipboard interlude. Duffy heard later that she had broken off her engagement to the big game hunter but has no idea whether it had anything to do with him. She made no attempt to contact him in neighbouring Tanganyika. But he did learn an important lesson: always lock the door.

Duffy took a bus from Mombasa to Arusha, in Tanganyika, as he had been told to, a jolting journey through the bush of some 200 miles. At Arusha he was met by George Muvenheimer, a large, genial figure full of Irish charm who piled him and his belongings into a battered Land Rover to drive the 40-odd miles to his farm on the lower slopes of Mount Meru. Duffy was discovering that distance and time meant little in Africa. But he was enchanted to be there: the emptiness, the sweeps of landscape – savannah, woodland, mountains and gorges; the new scents and sounds; and the wildlife that could be glimpsed even from a travelled road; the mysterious eyes picked up by the headlamps in the dark (Nightfall is early and sudden on the equator). He was far from London, far from the Scottish highlands. This was living.

At the dinner table that evening in the Muvenheimer homestead, it was still a new world. The room was lit by a Tilley lamp, not electricity (though a diesel generator provided electricity for the milking sheds). A tall, slender African man of impassive inky-black countenance waited at table in a spotless white smock and red fez, making scarcely a sound as he glided about. At the table were Muvenheimer, his German wife, their two young sons and the wife's German mother. They were having roast duck. Duffy felt strange, awkward, very much on edge. He was anxious not to put a foot wrong in these new surroundings.

"Here, try dis on your meat," said Muvenheimer, passing Duffy a bottle of Tomango tomato sauce. "It's very good. But you have to shake de bottle hard, it's very thick."

Duffy shook the bottle hard, to and fro. Unfortunately somebody had already unscrewed the lid and he managed to splash tomato sauce all over the shirt front of his host and new employer; also over his host and new employer's mother-in-law, the old German lady. Duffy wanted the earth to swallow him up.

But they all roared with laughter. The old German lady in particular was screeching with mirth. Duffy noticed with fascinated horror that one of her front teeth was loose and the more she laughed the more it wiggled. It was horrible.

Then the old lady started to choke, she was laughing so much. "Bang her on the back!" shouted Muvenheimer. Duffy got up and delivered a mighty whack. The loose tooth flew out of her mouth and into her bowl of soup.

This was Duffy's introduction to Africa. Was it an omen?

***

It was not quite Twickenham. The rugby field at Dodoma consisted mainly of baked earth and occasional tufts of grass. It was mid-winter and the drought had been severe. But the atmosphere was there; music from the police band and the governor walking out to meet the lined up players in all his ostrich-plumed glory, preceded by a police askari with raised sword, knife-edge creases in his knee-length shorts and gleaming boots. This was the epitome of empire. It was Tanganyika's Northern Province (headquartered in Arusha) versus the Southern Province (headquartered in Dodoma). Duffy was playing left wing for Northern Province. From this clash, Tanganyika's national side would be chosen, to take on such teams as Oxford University in warm-up games before they travelled on to Rhodesia and South Africa.

Northern Province beat Southern that day. Duffy was selected for the national side and was to play for them on several occasions. But what really struck him was the way, after being personally introduced to every player, the governor then called for a minute's silence. The players and the crowd of a few thousand bowed their heads. It was a mark of respect for the Southern Province fullback, who had been eaten by cannibals of the Maconde tribe.

The Maconde are a fierce people who live on both sides of the Rovuma River, which divides Tanganyika (as it then was known – today it is Tanzania) from Mozambique. The Maconde file their teeth to sharp points. Their faces are ornamentally scarred. In just a few years from that day they would launch a rebellion against Portuguese colonial rule in Mozambique – the first attack being with bow and arrow – which was to ultimately succeed as communist China supplied modern armaments, training in guerrilla warfare and political education in Marxism/Leninism. But this incident had occurred in British-ruled territory and it is not known if there was any political motive.

The victim had been a land surveyor whose Land Rover and equipment were found abandoned in Maconde territory. Police investigations led them to a village where they found a set of dentures in a cooking pot, which matched the surveyor's own dental record.

It was a sad affair and a setback for the Southern Province rugby side. This most definitely was not Twickenham. But it was the Africa that Duffy had dreamed of.

***

It was the final years of Britain's colonial empire in Africa. Harold MacMillan, the British Prime Minister, had spoken in South Africa's parliament of the winds of change that were sweeping down the continent. Ghana, on the west coast, had already been granted independence; the count-down was beginning in every colonial territory. But for the colonials — some of them settlers, some safari operators, some technicians and the people who drove the machinery of the colonial service, life went on much as before. Pink gins were served under sunshades on the lawn at midday to exquisitely turned out ladies and gentlemen by the legions of red-fezzed servants. Everyone dressed formally for dinner in the evenings. You could not hope to be admitted to a nightclub or hotel in Arusha or Nairobi without full evening dress. Life continued in a colonial bubble, the swirlings and intrigues of African nationalism and the demand for uhuru seemingly remote. The young set led an active, hedonistic lifestyle. Nairobi was some 250 miles away, across the border in Kenya, and Duffy and his crowd thought nothing of making the trip for a social weekend, usually putting up at a place called Slater House, where the young set gathered and were accommodated in chalets set in spacious grounds.

Here too, the dress code also was strictly formal, full evening dress in the bar and dining room. The young fellows and the girls would walk down from their chalets through the tropical evening, the men in their best bib and tucker, the girls in swirls of the latest fashion. It could go on a bit in the bar, and one night a certain fellow, resplendent in evening dress, was very much under the weather as a group of men strolled outside to answer the call of nature. The girls always retired in demure, lady-like fashion to the facilities provided. As everywhere in colonial Africa, the men spurned such fripperies and strolled out onto the lawn to answer the call al fresco, in a companionable group under the stars. It had always been so. The fellow who had been over-imbibing was having trouble with his zipper and was swaying badly. So while one of his companions held him steady by the shoulders, another kindly assisted with the zipper.

Now this individual had also brought with him a banana from the supper table. The zipper undone, it seemed a good idea to insert the banana, at which the inebriate took himself in hand (or so he thought) and blessed relief followed. Then followed the strange and unpleasant sensation of warmth and wetness in his superbly cut dress trousers. At the customary shake, the banana fell to the floor and, with a cry of anguish at what had befallen him, the poor fellow rushed off into the dark and to his chalet. He was not seen again that weekend, nor for a long time at Slaters. The night echoed to peals of female laughter in the bar as the story got about.

***

The quest for entertainment and female company at times became desperate. One evening Duffy was with friends in the coffee-growing south when word came through of a splendid party to be held at Moshe, far in the north at the foot of Kilimajaro. Undaunted by the 300 miles that lay ahead, three of them jumped into a Land Rover and set out. They realised they would get to the party late, so decided to get in to the swing of things on the way. They stopped at a duka and bought themselves a bottle apiece of Cinzano. This, they reckoned, should get them in a party mood. They also stopped when a Thompson's gazelle showed itself at the roadside, reached for a rifle and brought it down. They would bring victuals to the party as well. As they drove through the bush after nightfall, which had fallen like a curtain the way it does in the tropics, they swigged liberally from the Cinzano, which was not entirely to anyone's taste, but was at least alcohol (Duffy had by now lapsed from his earlier abstemious ways).

On arrival at the party they were the life and soul for about 20 minutes, though rubbery on their legs. They woke around 3 am, having slept where they dropped. The place was dark and silent, the party was most definitely over. They were due back at work. In four hours. It was time to leave. Duffy got behind the wheel of the Land Rover. The other two climbed into the back, threw themselves down beside the carcass of the buck and immediately began snoring. Duffy started the engine, switched on the lights and set off.

He was not in good shape for driving. The road through the bush was rough and winding. The Land Rover's seat seemed to have lost traction on his backside, he was sliding about. Came a sharp turn to the left and he spun the wheel. As he lurched to the right when the vehicle swung left, the door flung open and Duffy pitched out head first into the darkness. He sat up dazed at the roadside. The Land Rover, stout vehicle and pride of British automotive engineering, was ploughing on through the bush, down what turned out to be a long incline. He could hear thumps and crashes as the Land Rover made contact with the scrub bush. Once he glimpsed its tail lights as the rear of the vehicle bucked high in the air. Then there was a resounding crash and silence as the motor cut. He made his way through the darkness, following the trail of flattened shrubs, assisted by a quarter moon that was in the sky.

Suddenly the bulk of the Land Rover loomed before him. It appeared to be on its side, having collided with a large acacia. Then he heard the sound of snoring. At least his companions were alive. Inside, he managed to find a torch. He roused the other two, who were slightly indignant at being disturbed in their slumber. Then they saw they were covered in blood and began to panic. But it turned out the blood came from the carcass of the buck. They managed to heave the Land Rover back on its wheels. It started. They threaded their way through the bush, up the incline to the road. A magnificent vehicle is the Land Rover.

All three were decidedly the worse for wear when they reported for duty later that morning. But they were on time.

***

A Land Rover might be one thing, but there's nothing like a sports car to impress the girls. A sports car is hardly the ideal vehicle for East Africa. Its suspension is too low for the rough roads. An open car or canvas soft top is simply crazy in country inhabited by lions, leopards and other creatures with which you would rather not share its jauntiness. But a sports car does pull the girls. If there is one sports car that is totally unsuited to conditions in East Africa, it is the Morgan, an especially low-slung monster designed for the macadamed roadways and lanes of the English shires. But if there is one sports car that pulls the girls almost like a magnet, it is the Morgan.

A second-hand Morgan was advertised for sale in Nairobi. A friend and workmate simply had to have it. He, Duffy and two others drove across from Moshe, paid and drove the car out of the dealership. Seduction on wheels. They got on the road back to Tanganyika.

The low-slung Morgan was coping reasonably well with the roads, though you had to be careful and take it very slowly at times. There were four of them in the car. It was late afternoon and they should be back at Moshe in time to parade the car at the club, not least for the girls. Then, in a remote bit of bush country, the engine suddenly spluttered and died. There was plenty of fuel. When they lifted the bonnet, nothing obvious seemed wrong with the workings of the engine. This was serious. The problem required expertise better than they could muster. It was humiliating to be stranded with a Morgan like this.

Then they waved down a farm truck. The driver agreed to take three of them to the next town, where they would seek the assistance of a mechanic. The fourth would stay behind with the Morgan, whose gleaming beauty seemed ironic in the late afternoon sunlight.

They found a mechanic. He piled them all into his truck and they drove back to where they had left the Morgan and their friend. By the time they got there it was already dark. The Morgan was picked up by the headlights as it stood there. Sniffing at the car at the driver's door was a lioness. Other lionesses surrounded the Morgan. They went cold. Whatever had become of their pal? Had the lions made a meal of him? Horrors! They shouted at the lionesses, they banged on the sides of their vehicle. The lionesses sulkily gave way and went off into the bush.

There was real alarm now. Then a squeak came from under the Morgan. It was the missing one, safe enough but frightened out of his wits. Somehow he had managed to squeeze his bulky frame under the low-slung Morgan when the lions made their appearance. Back at the mechanical workshop next morning, he tried to show them how he had managed. He could not do it.

Yes, the Morgan pulls the girls. But those girls might turn out to be of the species Panthera leo.

***

Duffy had been in Tanganyika four years when he decided to move on. His year on the Muvenheimer farm at Mount Meru had brought him into daily contact with the African farmworkers. He was fluent in Swahili and related well to them. He had learned the ropes of dairy and mixed farming in East Africa. He had progressed to coffee planting and processing in the south of the country, which had been his intention all along. He had integrated in every way with colonial social life. He paid particular attention to the daughters of planters, safari operators and British colonial servants, who brought charm and excitement to the otherwise rough and ready surroundings.

Something of a scallywag in such matters, he generally had two or three girls in a relationship at one time. Twice he had relationships with sisters, who did not know of the double connection. Duffy is silent about such affairs while they are in progress, almost reclusive. He believes in limited commitment, no false promises. But a certain distance as well, however intimate the relationship. He finds safety in numbers. The ideal number of girlfriends at a time, he maintains, is three. Two, and you're spending too much time with each. (One, and you might as well be married). Four is too many to handle, too much to keep quiet. Three is ideal.

Duffy is not a political animal. He had no interest whatever in the politics of Britain. He had no views on the desirability or otherwise of a colonial empire; no opinion on the morality of it or otherwise. He was attracted to the colour and vibrancy of Africa, the opportunity for adventure. He was attracted by the idea of farming coffee in exotic surroundings. When he encountered a colonial society, he simply slotted into it for better or worse. When the stirrings of uhuru were felt, he wondered whether the lifestyle he had adopted was about to disappear. He had a long conversation with an old farmhand.

"What is this uhuru? Why do you want it."

"It is freedom for my people."

"Freedom? What freedom does it give you that you don't have already?"

The old chap thought for a bit. "We have freedom to decide which side of the road we want to drive."

Duffy had for some time been toying with the idea of going to the

Orient to acquire skills in the martial arts, which fascinated him. It might be an idea to first take a look at the African territories to the south. As with colonialism, he knew little or nothing of the issues at play in Rhodesia and Mozambique and had no position on them. He knew virtually nothing of Afrikaner nationalism in South Africa and the very strong moral questions surrounding the nationalists' doctrine of apartheid. Again he had no position, for or against.

But he did have a strong position against marriage. He saw it as an imprisonment. Yet his relationship with one of the Moshe girls was moving in that direction, for all his wiles. It was a disturbing unknown that was bearing down, a bit like uhuru. He decided it was time to take a look at the south before moving on to Japan. An American friend shared his enthusiasm for the martial arts and they arranged to meet up in Durban, South Africa's main harbour city. He resigned as a coffee plantation junior manager and took a ship at Mombasa, this time heading south into the Mozambique channel.

TANGANYIKA

Duffy had made a lot of friends during his years in Tanganyika, many of them from the rugby club, and they turned out in force to see him off from Mombasa. They had a somewhat riotous lunch in a restaurant, followed by a pub-crawl of the more rackety dockside establishments. Then they stood on the quay drinking quarts of Tusker beer, and Duffy only just made it up the gangplank of the Europa as the crew made ready to cast off. Light-headed, he checked in with the purser and was shown to his cabin, where he climbed into a top bunk and fell asleep.

He woke to a gentle rolling and the throb of the engines. They were at sea. He felt the call of nature, found the heads (as they term the toilets at sea) then came back to the cabin, where he undressed, climbed back onto the top bunk and was thinking vaguely that he ought to find out where the dining rooms were, as he was becoming hungry again, then went back to sleep, lying there in only his underpants.

He was rudely awakened by a stranger shaking him by the shoulders and yelling at him in voluble Italian. The cabin light was on. Standing in a corner wearing only a nightdress was a woman (stunningly beautiful as it happened) with a look of utter horror on her face. The man (who turned out to be her husband) started swinging wild punches at Duffy, who then jumped down and gave him a couple of hard ones back. The woman was screaming, Duffy and the stranger wrestled and punched. Other strangers joined the melee from the passageway outside. Then a burly ship's officer was on the scene and he wrestled the two apart and quietened things. He led Duffy back to the correct cabin.

It turned out the Italian couple had also joined the ship at Mombasa. The woman had been tired and turned in early, taking the bottom bunk. Her husband went to watch a film in one of the lounges. Duffy misread the cabin numbers after his jaunt to the heads, went into the wrong cabin, undressed and climbed onto the top bunk where he lay stretched out resplendent in nothing but a pair of brief underpants. The husband had a drink or two at the bar after the film then came down to the cabin to discover an all but naked man in the top bunk, above his wife. Then all hell broke loose, Italian honour and machismo at stake. The husband was not having a good night because he got decidedly the worst of it in the scrap with Duffy, who was rugby-fit and farm life fit and had an interest in the martial arts anyway. As Duffy was led away, the husband's eye had closed completely and his wife (who turned out to be perhaps the most beautiful woman on board) was still having hysterics. For all concerned, it was an inauspicious start to the voyage.

The Europa was a superbly graceful passenger ship of the Italian Lloyd-Tristieno Line. She and her identically white-hulled sister ship, the Africa, plied between the east coast of Africa and the ports of Italy and elsewhere in southern Europe, via the Suez Canal.

Whenever they passed at sea, inevitably steaming in different directions, one outward the other inward-bound, there would be a dignified ceremony of recognition, signals flying from the halyards, hooting on the ships' sirens. This was the heyday of post-war passenger shipping and Lloyd-Tristieno were fully part of it. Below decks punch-ups in the passenger quarters were certainly not part of the tradition.

Next day they were sailing into Dar-es-Salaam, Tanganyika's main port and a colourful and romantic touching point of Africa and the Arab world. The name is Arabic and means Haven of Peace. But the name was illusory on this occasion. As they sailed into harbour, a helicopter flew overhead. It was carrying Royal Marines from a warship on patrol in the Indian Ocean, on their way to suppress an army mutiny in the newly independent country. This they achieved in record time and with zero casualties on either side, by lobbing a few thunderflashes into the mutineers' barracks, at which they surrendered. Then Duffy encountered on deck an individual whose attitude was immediately hostile and insulting.

"Hey you, you stand-a up when you speak-a to me!" It was another Italian, dressed in an immaculate cream-coloured suit.

"I beg your pardon? Who the hell are you?"

"I show you!" he said, adopting an old-fashioned boxing stance, fists clenched. He seemed to be trying to impress the females present (It transpired that he had actually been involved in the cabin fracas the previous evening).

This was provocation too far. Duffy gave him one in the kisser, as they say in the classics, and blood spurted immediately from mashed lips, all over the cream suit. He gave him a couple more before crewmen intervened and dragged them apart. The incident was observed by dozens of passengers. Among most of them Duffy became an instant hero and they rallied round and offered him drinks. Later that afternoon he was playing table tennis on deck when an officer approached.

"Il Capitano, he wanta see you."

Duffy was led to a suite off the officers' quarters where Il Capitano was seated, his officers ranged on either side. It had all the appearance of a drumhead court martial. But Duffy noticed that a couple of the officers seemed to be struggling to keep a straight face.

"Why you fight-a with the other passengers? Two black eye now. One bleeding mouth. Why? They pay-a same money as you, why you can't-a leave them alone?"

Duffy protested his peaceable nature. "Everyone keeps picking on me, I don't pick on them. I'm a lover, not a fighter."

"Ah, maybe that-a the problem."

He was led away and heard no more of it.

Then they were in Beira, anchored out in the channel off Mozambique's second-largest port. This was Portuguese Africa, not even a colony in terms of the doctrine of the Salazar regime in Lisbon but an integral province of Metropolitan Portugal. Duffy had never been to the Portuguese territories before and was eager to go ashore. A ship the size of Europa stayed out in the deepwater channel, not tying up at the dockside, and the immigration authorities boarded from a launch and stamped the passports of all who wished to go ashore. But Duffy had been flirting with some Rhodesian girls on board and missed all that. To his great disappointment, when the harbour ferry drew alongside to take passengers ashore, he was not allowed to board because his passport had not been stamped. There he was, all dressed up in a natty American lightweight suit, but nowhere to go. And all his fellow-passengers who were any fun were being ferried ashore.

Standing disconsolately at the rail and looking at the early evening lights of Beira, he noticed a barge alongside, pumping water supplies to the ship. A rope tied it to the ship's rail. That barge obviously must return to the docks. Years of obstacle courses and outdoor resourcefulness at Gordonstoun paid off. He shinned down the rope, landing on the deck in his natty suit, to the astonishment of the barge crew. But they understood Swahili and agreed to take him ashore when they were finished.

It was late by the time the barge arrived at an obscure part of the docks. Duffy found a taxi to take him to the red light district, and soon enough met up with his chums from the ship. An evening of revelry ensued as they moved from bar to bar, night club to night club, eventually availing themselves of a brothel before they decided to call it a night. (In the Portuguese territories this was de rigeur for a night on the town). It was by then 3 am. After a taxi ride to the ferry point, Duffy and his sole companion by that stage discovered to their consternation that between them they had only enough for one ticket. They spun a coin to decide who would take the ferry and who would swim. Duffy lost. He took off his shoes and handed them to his companion. "I'll see you tomorrow on the ship."

Then he dived into the tepid waters of Beira in his natty American lightweight suit and struck out for the Europa, whose lights were riding several hundred yards distant. He made fair progress. He was not to know it at the time, but it was ebb tide when the notorious currents of Beira harbour go temporarily still as they start changing direction. He did not even think about sharks. The beaches of Kenya and Tanganyika are protected from them by coral. But not so off Beira. The place is infested with sharks, attracted by the detritus of a port city. Temporarily part of that detritus, Duffy splashed about as the Europa loomed above him.

Swimming out to a ship is all very well, but how do you get aboard? Do you climb up the anchor chain? Then Duffy saw the lights of a small craft alongside. It was the same barge that had taken him ashore earlier, returned with more provisions. He hailed the crew in Swahili. They greeted him like a long-lost brother and hauled him out of the water. The barge was drawn up at an open hatch in the ship's hull, where the supplies were being taken aboard. Duffy heaved himself aboard as well, dripping wet and in a once natty American lightweight suit. "I'm from Cabin 1513" he told the totally astonished petty officer on duty at the hatchway. He let him pass.

At lunch next day a well-rested Duffy was approached in the dining room by a junior officer he had befriended. "Tell-a me," the officer began nervously, "They say-a you swim out to da ship last night?"

"Yes, that's true."

The officer leaped in the air with a whoop of delight "I mak-a da be-e-e-g money! I win-a da bet!" The story of Duffy's escapade had got around. Most of the officers pooh-poohed it, saying it was impossible. This officer had bet them it was true. He was in the money.

Il Capitano was a man of relaxed manner, a mariner dedicated to his ship, his men and his passengers. But this had been a difficult voyage. There had been the unpleasant incidents of fighting between passengers. A near-riotous party spirit had also developed. Il Capitano was familiar with shipboard parties and shipboard romantic flings. He was a man of the world. But this voyage had been very testing. A group of passengers had taken to drinking and playing the piano in the saloon into the early hours of the morning. The purser had been obliged only last night to lock up the piano to get them to disperse. There were limits.

They were approaching Durban. Some of the more riotous of the passengers were to disembark here, including the troublesome one who had been involved in the fighting and, he was told, had gone ashore illegally in Beira then swum back to the ship. He was trouble. But normality would prevail. Il Capitano was on the bridge. In a couple of hours he would salute his sister ship, the Africa, as they passed mid-morning. The mate had personally checked that the correct signals were on the halyard in the flag locker.

The two graceful ships practically glided toward each across the clean blue waters off the Tongaland coast of Natal, Europa steaming south, Africa steaming north. Il Capitano stood on the bridge wing and saluted his counterpart, less than half a mile away, as both vessels' sirens gave two deep hoots of greeting. His counterpart would be doing the same. This was the tradition of the sea. The Africa was resplendent with the usual flag signals of recognition and congratulation. So was the Europa.

But then Il Capitano's counterpart on the Africa called suddenly for a telescope. Flying proud on the Europa's halyard were two unusual signals: a pair of woman's panties and a woman's brassiere. That is what happens when you lock up the piano and force people to look for amusement in the flag locker.

DURBAN

Duffy stepped ashore in Durban for a holiday of a few weeks, waiting for an American he had met in Tanganyika. The arrangement was that they would set off for Japan to train in karate, which fascinated them both. Durban meanwhile was a pleasant place for a restful interlude. Its sub-tropical climate and vegetation, its beaches, its warm, swimmable surf and its multicultural vibrancy had made it South Africa's premier holiday resort, served by a range of quality hotels and restaurants. This holiday ambience co-existed with the constant maritime bustle of its being Africa's largest and busiest port, giving it another facet. Durban was known to seafarers as the liveliest port of call by far on the east coast of Africa.

But the interlude dragged on. The American failed to rendezvous. Duffy managed to contact him and, to his concern, was told he was otherwise involved. He had not considered the Japan trip a fixed arrangement. Duffy was on his own. What were his options? Go on to Japan alone? Return to Tanganyika? Return to Britain? (This he rejected after the most fleeting consideration). He was lying on South Beach one morning considering his options when a beach photographer approached. Where had he come from, the photographer asked, noting his deep tan. Duffy told him East Africa. Ah, that explained it. They got to discussing the lusciousness of the girls disporting themselves on the beach. A beach photographer, Duffy was told, scored better with the girls than the lifeguards. These bronzed, muscled heroes operated between the bathing beacons and nowhere else. Photographers had the run of the whole beach, and they got into conversation with every girl they approached professionally. The results could be spectacular because working girls on holiday from the Transvaal and the Free State were after fun. Duffy found this fascinating.

Then his new acquaintance confided that he wanted to take a few weeks' holiday. Before he could go he needed to find a replacement. Could Duffy handle a camera? Would he be interested? And in this way Duffy was launched on a career that was to last another 40 years and more. Durban was to become not just a temporary interlude but his home and headquarters.

Duffy took to beach photography. His new acquaintance had not exaggerated. He discovered that people were absolutely creatures of habit, they went to the same spot on the same beach every day. If a girl caught your fancy, she was bound to be there every day and you could chat to her and photograph her. He got to know the sleeping quarters of hotels up and down the beachfront.

But soon he graduated from beachfront photography. Durban throbbed with night spots and restaurants. It was a cosmopolitan sector that was beginning to boom. Duffy was part of that boom. He took a position with John Cousin, a retired British South Africa Police officer who ran a social pictures service that prided itself on quality and swiftness of delivery. Duffy in his immaculate tuxedo became a familiar figure in all the nights spots and eateries. He also befriended staff and management, developing a knowledge and skill with the most exotic cuisines and wines that has never left him.

There was the occasional small jolt in this idyllic existence. Duffy had three encounters with the police, two of which involved overnight stays in the accommodation provided. One lunch time he met up with a BOAC pilot, some air hostesses and a Durban attorney named Ivan Isaacs at a restaurant just off the beachfront, owned by a volcanically temperamental Italian, Enrico Ferrari, who was known to chase diners out of his restaurant brandishing a revolver if they complained about anything.

They had ordered but barely tasted their starters when some kind of altercation with the waiter occurred. Next thing Ferrari had rushed out of the kitchen and was screaming at them to get out of his restaurant. They left in some embarrassment without paying – they hadn't been given the chance to eat their meal – and went on to the Oysterbox at Umhlanga Rocks, where they forgot the disturbance with an excellent and well-lubricated lunch.

A few nights later Duffy was at *La Popote* restaurant near Ferrari's place in his tuxedo and with his camera. He was busy with his patter when he got touched on the arm. It was a small spindly man in a beige safari suit – the short pants version with beige stockings – and the small moustache that often goes with such an outfit.

"I want to speak to you."

"Who are you?"

"I'm from the CID at Point police station."

Duffy looked down his nose at him. "I thought you were a boy scout."

At which the little fellow took umbrage and snapped the handcuffs on him. Duffy was flung into a police van and taken to Point police station and charged with bilking. Ferrari had laid a charge after the incident of the meal not eaten and not paid for. Duffy in his tuxedo was by far the best-dressed in the overnight holding cell. His fellow prisoners were doing things like adjusting the razor blades stitched into their blue denims and surreptitiously puffing at dagga zols. It was smelly in the cell and hot as Hades. He was relieved to be able to telephone John Cousin — who was panicking over the non-arrival of Duffy's spools of film from the night before — to get him to come along and arrange bail.

When it came to court Isaacs, who had been at the non-lunch at Ferrari's , defended the case, producing the receipts for the successful lunch at Umhlanga — the same day, the same lunch hour — to prove what had really happened. (But it did not deter Ferrari. He was to subsequently himself appear in court for menacing customers with a revolver. The Durban of the 1960s seemed to abound with eccentrics).

The old XL tea lounge had been a meeting point at South Beach for generations. It stood on a high point, looking down on the beach itself and all the beachfront shops and kiosks. It was where Duffy met up one late afternoon with a group of friends, some of them from East Africa, to plan the evening ahead. The XL was what its name stated. It had no liquor licence. Whatever Durban's inclination, it had to abide by the strict Calvinism imposed by Pretoria. But how could an evening be planned without lubrication? Duffy had brought with him a gallon jar of wine (ridiculously cheap in those days) and the group called for glasses and made merry until a police van that was cruising past stopped and spoiled the party.

A couple of humourless konstabels herded them all, girls and boys, into the Black Maria and took them to Point police station, where Duffy began to feel he was acquiring some kind of status as a frequent customer. There they were to be charged with drinking in public. (Something absolutely taboo in those days. You could get paralytic in a street bar but that was all right – there were bricks and mortar between you and the innocents on the street). But fortunately there was on the desk that night a middle-aged sergeant who had seen it all and knew when the law was being ridiculous. He quashed it and told them to move on.

This had been no more than a glancing encounter with the forces of law and order, yet the evening ended with one of the XL tea lounge revellers having to have his eye and forehead stitched at Addington hospital, which is also in the Point precinct. After being released from Point police station, the group made for a party in the upmarket suburb of La Lucia, north of Durban. Things were hectic: loud music, dancing, bowls of potent punch. But they were short on glasses. Duffy made do with a milk bottle – one of the heavy glass ones. He was sitting on a wall on the outside verandah, drinking punch from the milk bottle, when he noticed numbers were thinning as it grew later. A proper glass would by now be available in the kitchen. Duffy threw the milk bottle backwards over his shoulder into the darkness and made for the kitchen.

Outside in the darkness, one of his friends from Tanganyika was lying on the front lawn with a girl, doing slightly improper things. He was just removing her bra when a universe of blazing lights suddenly exploded in his head.

Duffy emerged from the kitchen to find another friend from Tanganyika – brother of the one who had been out on the lawn – causing a scene. Who had done this to his brother, he demanded to know. The brother had blood pouring from cuts about the eye and forehead. They milled about in confusion, nobody owning up. Then somebody pointed out that the lad needed stitches. It was only when they were driving back to the Point precinct, to Addington Hospital, and the victim explained what had happened that Duffy went cold, realising he was the culprit. Sheepishly he owned up. But they saw the funny side, the victim included. To this day at board meetings in Durban – he was to become a driving force in local business – people often wonder where he picked up those awful scars.

That same ex-Tanganyikan was to feature in another Duffy encounter with the police, also in the setting of the Point precinct. Duffy was sharing a flat in London House, which ran between Smith and West Streets, in the central business district. He was driving a 1929 Chevrolet coupe. Late one night, he and a group of boys and girls – including the scarred Tanganyikan – had repaired to Addington beach to skinnydip. They were disporting themselves in the surf when Duffy decided enough was enough, it was time for bed. He walked up the beach and got into the Chev. There seemed little point in donning his entire tuxedo so he put on his underpants

– a very brief cut known as "skants" – and tuxedo jacket for the drive back. Arrived at the open parking lot near London House, he noticed for the first time that the others seemed also to have put their clothes in his car. It was late and Duffy was befuddled. He realised he could not leave the clothes in the back of an open coupe; they would get stolen. He would take them to his flat. They all knew where he lived. Somebody would give them a lift.

He rolled the clothing into a ball. A woman's bra he put over his head, knotting it under his chin, the cups pulled down like earmuffs. He was strolling through the city centre toward London House – tuxedo top, skants, a bra as earmuffs and a bundle of other clothing under his arm – when a police patrol van came by. Here surely was something worthy of investigation.

The konstabel challenged him in Afrikaans. Duffy replied in voluble Swahili. Both konstabels then bundled him into the back of the van and took him to Smith Street police station.

Meanwhile, the rest of the skinnydipping party at Addington beach were in dismay. Duffy was gone. Their clothes were gone. Where could they be? They waited. They shivered. No Duffy. If they were in a predicament now, what would it be with the dawn when the beachfront stirred into life and they were still huddled there, starkers? They had to make a move. All lived miles away in the suburbs. Duffy's flat in the central business district was the only place to head for. But in the nude?

One girl had stowed her clothes somewhere away from Duffy's car. But one girl's gear doesn't go very far in clothing a party of eight or so. If Duffy's two konstabels had gone out on patrol again, they would have encountered something even stranger than a figure in skants, tuxedo and earmuffs fashioned from a bra. A group of skimpily clothed to stark naked boys and girls were flitting from doorway to doorway through the Point precinct; progressing past the city hall and into the central business district; and from there into London House, where they took a lift.

Duffy's flatmate woke to the doorbell ringing insistently. He was totally astonished to find on the doorstep a posse of nudists who tumbled through as he opened up, loudly demanding the whereabouts of Duffy.

But of course Duffy was not there. He was in a cell at the Smith Street police station, still in his tuxedo top and skants. He had been kicking at the cell door and shouting. He was told to shut up, but after that there had been no response. He looked about his surroundings. The cell had one of those squat toilets with a cistern for flushing. He investigated the cistern and found there was a split-pin in the flushing mechanism. He removed it and water immediately started gushing everywhere, not letting up. It covered the cell floor, several inches deep. It ran under the door. He could hear it splashing down stairs. Yells of indignation came from the other cells.

By dawn the entire cell area was flooded. Duffy resumed his banging on the door. Two furious konstabels arrived and took him into the charge office.

"You're in big trouble!"

Duffy had a terrible hangover and had not slept all night. But he managed to get some fun out of it.

"Your name?"

He slurred something unintelligible, feigning complete drunkenness.

"Say again! Your name?"

He slurred again, but eventually they got it out of him. Height? Weight? He had a lot of fun with that.

Then: "Are those your own teeth?"

"No, I borrowed them for the weekend."

"Don't get funny, hey! What car do you drive?"

"1929 Chev."

"I warned, you, don't get funny!"

And so it went on. They asked where he worked. He gave the name of John Cousin. A policeman telephoned him.

"Where is he?" Cousin was again worried about the non-appearance of the spools.

"The Smith Street police cells."

"Oh no, not again!"

This was not a helpful comment. The police now thought they had on their hands a hardened criminal whose record had to be investigated.

Duffy was charged with the theft of all the clothes he had with him – including his own trousers. The flooding of the police station they couldn't manage to actually pin on him, though they were mightily suspicious. John Cousin arrived to pick up his spools. The police began to realise Duffy's account of things just might be true. The day wore on. The police said they would drop the charge of theft if every individual came in and identified each item of clothing as his or her own. There was much telephoning. Some of the police were struggling to keep a straight face as the skinnydipping girls and boys came in and picked out this bra, that pair of knickers and that pair of skants as belonging to themselves. It was late in the day before Duffy was released.

He'd had no sleep. Neither he nor his tuxedo were fit for service that night. So he took the night off and had his tuxedo cleaned and pressed. Next night he was back on his rounds.

Next Duffy branched out on his own and things seemed to go from strength to strength. The money was good, his reputation was high with people right across the hospitality and entertainment industry. The quality of his work was so good, and the delivery so prompt, that many restaurateurs came to see his regular presence as a drawcard. He was living in a three-storey mock Tudor house in Morningside with a group of architecture students he had met and befriended in Tanganyika. Life as a social photographer was good.

But a cloud appeared on the horizon. A girl from Tanganyika got in touch. She was coming down to Durban, expressly to see him. He heard the ominous chimes of wedding bells. She would be arriving on the Union Castle cruise liner, Rene del Mar, from Mombasa.

Why Duffy should have contrived to leave Durban on the same vessel she arrived on is open to conjecture. But he booked a ticket for himself for the next cruising leg to Cape Town. He stayed out of sight and incognito when the ship docked and boarded only at the last minute so there could be no awkward encountering of the lady. This was hairsbreadth escape. It is only two days' sailing from Durban to Cape Town so Duffy travelled light. Besides, he intended restocking his wardrobe while in Cape Town, which in the mid-1960s was the centre of clothing fashion.

Duffy had been to sea on the Uganda, then the Europa. But the size and sophistication of the Rene del Mar – her size and luxury – plus the shipboard entertainment and riotous fun told Duffy an extended cruise would be fun. The ship went on from Cape Town to Brazil and Argentina, then back to Cape Town. He made inquiries at the purser's office. There was no such thing as a credit card in those days; you paid cash. He had enough with him to pay for the rest of the trip because of the extra he had brought to pay for a shopping spree. But it would leave him with only about a pound a day to spend on board ship, for several weeks. Even taking into account money values in those days, and the fact that drinks at the bar were duty-free out at sea, he would be on a very tight budget. Also, he did not have his passport with him.

Arrived in Cape Town, he had little time to stop and admire the magnificent Table Mountain with its tablecloth of white mist dropping from its sides as he hurried ashore to find a telephone. He got hold of one of his architecture student housemates in Durban. He telephoned again in mid-afternoon. Yes, his housemate had managed to persuade one of the aircrew of a South African Airways flight to carry his passport to Cape Town and drop it off at a certain hotel. Duffy went back to the ship, booked and paid for his passage to Rio de Janeiro and Buenos Aires return. Then he went ashore again, did some last-minute shopping and picked up his passport from the hotel desk. The last-minute shopping was for a dozen bottles of Oude Meester brandy. Duffy calculated that if he was to imbibe on the trip, it would have to be from his cabin. He got back to the ship just in time to get up the gangplank before it was pulled away. He checked in at the purser's office.

"Your luggage, sir. Can we take it to your cabin?"

Duffy pointed to his bag with the twelve bottles of Oude Meester. The purser's clerk just shook his head and waved him on. Duffy was on a six weeks' cruise with a suit, two shirts and socks and underwear for two days. He had cabin laundry to do every night.

The Rene del Mar ploughed across the Atlantic, shipboard jollity and naughtiness all the way. Duffy would take a couple of slugs from his Oude Meester store every evening, then drink Coke at the ship's bars. He got on well with his five cabin-mates who had boarded in Cape Town. When they reached Rio, they went ashore and a couple of good-looking Brazilian girls – they called themselves "escorts of the day" – latched onto Duffy and one of his companions and took them on an extended tour of the entire city and surrounds, including the famous Corcovado with its enormous statue of Christ. Duffy and his friend wined and dined the girls all day – the friend paying because of Duffy's straitened circumstances – and eventually the foursome ended up in a poor district at what could be euphemistically termed a lodging house. Each was in bed with his girl when a commotion broke out. The place was being raided by the police. Boots were pounding about the corridors, girls screamed. Duffy and his friend took the first-floor window as an escape route, landing on the iron roof of a single-storey building next door. Duffy gashed his leg badly, ripping his suit, but somehow they managed to find their way down and escape on foot. Eventually they found a taxi that took them back to the ship. It was 2am. They had not paid for the girls' services nor for the lodging house. But it did not seem a good idea to go back. Until the police raid, the girls had been given a great day.

The Rene del Mar went on to Buenos Aires, then sailed on the return trip to Cape Town. And about this point Duffy's material fortunes changed. He had struck up a relationship with a gorgeous Greek girl from Johannesburg named Eva. This very wealthy young lady was alone in a honeymoon suit that had been booked by she and her fiancé. But the engagement had been broken off, there was no wedding. Rather than lose the deposit she had put down, Eva took the trip on her own. One thing led to another and very soon the honeymoon suite was being put to its intended use. From scrounging about living off a measure or two of Oude Meester every night, Duffy suddenly was in the lap of luxury. The return voyage was memorable.

They docked at Cape Town, where Table Mountain makes it probably the most scenically magnificent landfall in the world. Eva caught a flight to Johannesburg. (Though this was not to be the last he saw of her. In fact he was subsequently to also have an affair with her sister He could never make up; his mind which was the better lover). Duffy was almost flat broke. It took him three days to hitchhike from Cape Town to Durban, sleeping rough on the way. Eventually he got to his digs in Morningside, or rather to where his digs had been. The three-storey mock Tudor house had been burned to the ground, all his belongings with it. He had no idea where his student friends were to be found.

But he did still have his camera. He borrowed a tuxedo from a friend and that night started the rounds again as a social photographer.

THE CONGO

While Duffy had been planting coffee and partying in Tanganyika and taking photographs and partying in Durban, events in the former Belgian Congo had been building climactically into a political volcano. The independence process had been chaotic from the start. The vast country with its immense diversity of tribal, linguistic and regional interests became a nightmare of chaos and brutality as independence dawned, the Belgian colonial authorities having in no way adequately prepared the populace for any such thing. The anarchy was captured in an incident on independence day when King Baudouin, who attended the handing-over to an elected government, had his ceremonial sword snatched from its scabbard by an urchin who disappeared back into the crowd, waving it triumphantly as he went. It was a time of the Cold War, and the Congo had become a cockpit of fierce regional proxy conflict. With its fabulous mineral wealth and hydro-electric potential, the Congo was a worthwhile prize in the Cold War; also because of its geopolitical position in equatorial Africa, its sheer size and population and its symbolic value. It was a worthy prize for the communist bloc. It was as worth clinging on to for the non-communist capitalist world, notably Union Miniere, the giant Belgian mining group. Thousands of Belgian nationals living in the country were at risk. Thousands of nuns and missionaries were at risk. Various regions, notably the mineral-rich Katanga province, had opted for outright secession. There were all kinds of justifications for foreign intervention. The Belgian army intervened on several occasions to protect its nationals. Large numbers of Belgian troops had enlisted in the Force Publique, the independent Congo's new paramilitary gendarmerie. The United Nations intervened following a Security Council resolution. Foreign mercenary forces were raised to intervene.

As already noted, Duffy is not a political animal. Events in the Congo had interested him not at all. In Durban one morning he noticed that somebody had set up a desk in the city gardens in Smith Street, across the road from where he and a photographer colleague had set up offices. He strolled across to find out what it was about. He found a recruiting officer for a mercenary force that was being raised to fight in the Congo. The terms seemed very generous: £300 a month, half to be paid in the Congo, the rest at home, wherever home might be. In the mid-1960s, company executives were not earning that kind of money. But Duffy laughed at the idea. He had no military background at all; national service had been abolished in Britain. He was perfectly content with life as a photographer in Durban of the social and holiday whirl.

Then he heard from close friends from Tanganyika. Barney Carey and another fellow had been part of his rugby-playing, partying set. Both had enlisted with Five Commando, a mercenary unit that had been tasked by the government with assisting the Armee Nationale Congolais in bringing order to the chaos. They had completed a six-month contract and were in Johannesburg enjoying some leave before signing another contract. There was a fantastic party being thrown in a flat in Hillbrow. Why didn't Duffy come up for it?

It was a riotous party, to equal anything that happened in Tanganyika. Nearly all the men present were mercenaries down from the Congo. The conversation roared, anecdotes were embellished. The liquor flowed. This was the life.

Duffy stirred awake in his seat. He was decidedly fragile from the night before. The Dakota's motors droned, everything in the cabin seemed to vibrate. The aircraft bucked in a thermal updraft. "We're still four hours out from Albert," Barney Carey said from the seat beside him. "Best you get some kip while you can."

Duffy had signed on. It was not quite the Queen's shilling trick. He had been perfectly aware of what he was doing. It just seemed a fun thing to do. He told them he had served with the King's African Rifles (which he had not). But the recruiting officer with the forms had seemed more interested in his linguistic skills anyway. They wanted Swahili-speakers. That he certainly was. He drifted back to sleep again.

FIVE COMMANDO

Albertville (now called Kalemie) is a port on Lake Tanganyika that in the early 1960s still had a shipbuilding yard to serve the steamer traffic on the lake which, in the absence of proper roads in that part of the eastern Congo, served as a major internal transport artery for some 400 miles, as well as connecting the Congo with Tanganyika, which lay across the water to the east. By the time Duffy and his contingent got there, Albertville was in a reduced state. Much of the dockland was underwater due to an unanticipated rise of about five feet in the lake level over the years, while the town itself was shabby and half-abandoned. Traces of a former colonial splendour were still there in a bowling club and hotels and bars in the town, but the Belgians had almost all of them departed in the turmoil that accompanied independence and when the town was captured and held by Simba insurgents backed by the communist bloc, who went on to conduct a reign of terror. The only outsiders still operating there were a handful of Greek and Lebanese traders.

One of the first operations launched by Colonel Mike Hoare, a former commander of 5 Commando, had been to send in a flying column to drive the Simbas from Albertville, which he did with spectacular success. But the town was still caught up in the alarums of war. The Simbas held much of the lakeside bush; they still dominated and bullied the local villagers. They were armed with the ubiquitous AK-47s of guerrilla struggle in various theatres of the Cold War worldwide; also with heavy machineguns, RPG grenades and land mines. The materiel was brought across by dug-out canoe from bases in Tanganyika, and a major part of the mercenary operation was lake patrols at night in Swift gunboats (as used on a significant scale in Vietnam), brought in and assembled by operatives of the American Central Intelligence Agency, as well as fishing vessels that had been converted and armed. This was highly specialised – and often highly successful – naval activity in which Duffy's contingent did not participate, though they were often transported up and down the lake in naval craft.

Five Commando was now under Colonel John Peters (like Hoare, formerly in the British army) and the mission was to take further Hoare's success; consolidate in Albertville, take the fight to the Simbas in the bush and in the villages that were giving them shelter and clear that region of insurgency. It was difficult and dangerous and the work began virtually from the time they disembarked from the Dakota. They boarded a lake steamer and were taken about 100 miles northward to their camp at Baraka for two weeks of intensive training before they went on live missions. Then it was war in the bush and it was real.

Duffy coped well, in spite of his lack of formal military training. Several years in Tanganyika had taught him bushcraft and how to handle a rifle. And a mercenary operation was different from a formal military one; it relied not so much on discipline and well-oiled procedures and tactics as on the initiative of the individual. Also, Hoare (whose background in the Second World War had been with armour) had developed the tactic of the motorised flying column, which was especially effective in the Congo. Five Commando would gather accurate intelligence as to where the Simbas would be found; where their munitions were stashed; which villages were sheltering them.

Then a party would storm the place and inflict maximum casualties, always with the element of surprise, driving the Simba survivors into flight and driving home the message that it did not pay to consort with them. If it could be done with armoured cars rather than on foot, so much the better. The key to this was intelligence, which was why the recruiting agents had been so eager to sign up Swahili-speakers. Swahili was the lingua franca of the entire Great Lakes region.

War is a grim and ghastly business. There is no romance or glamour about it at all. It consists in killing people you do not know, before they get the chance to kill you, plus intimidating the waverers. The Congo was no different from Vietnam or any other theatre that was a proxy of the Cold War. The CIA orchestrated things from inside the Congo on behalf of President Mobutu, who was considered to be an ally of Western democracy. Operatives from the Soviet Union and China based themselves across the water in Tanganyika and orchestrated things inside the Congo to serve international revolution against what they termed imperialism, colonialism and capitalism. Ordinary civilians, who knew nothing of these issues, were caught in the crossfire. The Simbas would kidnap young men after bullying village headmen or schoolmasters to identify those who showed promise in their schoolwork. These would be ferried across the lake to Tanganyika for a further selection process. Some would proceed to Moscow and Peking. Those not selected would not return, they knew too much already and were expendable. Villages that were coerced into offering shelter and support to Simba guerrillas could expect harsh retaliation from Five Commando. It was brutal, nightmarish stuff.

This was to be Duffy's life for almost eighteen months. Contracts lasted six months. He signed on for two more. It was not like a regular army where there would be a rotation of frontline troops for rest and recuperation. Here the grind and the danger would be constant, relieved only very occasionally by a night in some forlorn bar. Some of his comrades in arms were from the rougher strata of society. Some turned out to be thorough bad eggs, psychopaths. It happens in any military force. But they were a minority. A camaraderie developed; there was a sense of achievement as they gradually got on top of the Simba rebellion and cleared the region of meaningful insurgency. Promotion came rapidly to those who showed initiative. On his first contract, Duffy became a sergeant. On his next a lieutenant, then a captain. And the money was good.

BLOWN UP

The scout vehicle bucked and lurched along the sand track in low gear, its high-revving engine and complaining transmission seemingly a telegraph to every Simba insurgent who might be lurking in the high grass and light woodland of this western shore of Lake Tanganyika. It was almost mid-morning and progress had been painfully slow along the track, only about eight miles. The patrol had to reach Firizi, another ten miles on, where 5 Commando had taken a key ridge and were holding it against Simba counter-attacks but were running low on ammunition. Then the patrol had to get all the way back to camp at Baraka before dark, otherwise their chances were slim. This was Simba territory and the odds tipped massively in favour of the insurgents after nightfall. The scout vehicle was not of the armoured, four-wheel drive variety used by conventional armies, it was a commandeered one-and-a-half-ton civilian truck with the windscreen, windows and doors removed and a 7.62mm heavy machinegun mounted behind the cab. Sid Cummings manned the machinegun, hanging on grimly as the vehicle bucked and swayed, scanning the surrounding grass and bush for the first spurts of smoke that would be followed a split second later by the crack-crack-crack! of AK47s if there were an ambush. Half a dozen men lurched uncomfortably about on the back, sharing the space with ammunition chests and a supply of firewood that was also being taken through. The group at Firizi were beginning to run out of the village furniture they had commandeered and chopped up for firewood when they took the place.

In front in the cab, Duffy and the driver were in a furious argument. The sand track consisted of two deep ruts caused by the passage of vehicles and a grassy ridge down the middle, so typical of African roads – the "middel mannetjie" of South African parlance. The driver, who was from the transport section, not the Wildcat section like the rest, stuck to the established wheelruts. Then when they reached the regular deep potholes, he would take the vehicle in excruciatingly slowly to take it through. This was a transport man concerned not to damage the vehicle. Duffy was furious. Not only was progress too slow, making the party a sitting duck in an ambush and certain not to get to Firizi, then back to Baraka before dark, this was no way to drive in an area known to be mined. The scout vehicle should be riding with two wheels on the middle mannetjie, two on the verge, straddling the established wheelruts and zig-zagging to avoid running onto any conventionally placed mine. The danger was real. So many landmines had detonated in that district in recent days that a detachment of sappers of the Armee National Congolaise had arrived by lake at Baraka to begin a sweep to lift mines and clear the roads. They had set up camp nearby. But the driver was stubborn and Duffy had to give him an ultimatum. "Look, I'm the officer. If you don't do what I say, I'm going to put you in the back and get somebody else to drive. Do you want to lose face?"

Sulkily, the driver began zig-zagging and riding the middel mannetjie and straddling the established ruts wherever he could. They had been travelling about two minutes in this mode when suddenly the truck lifted into the air with a dull boom. Duffy and his driver found themselves flying through the air in what seemed like a kind of slow-motion; so did machinegunner Cummings and his companions on the back. There was no flash – that happens only in the films – just a dull, heavy percussion, G-forces then a hard landing. The truck was on its side. One man was dead, three badly wounded. The truck had caught the landmine with a rear wheel in the zig-zag, the main force of the explosion missing the occupants. In the driver's previous mode of riding in the ruts, everyone would have been killed. Desperately the party got the heavy machinegun off its mountings and set it up; scrambled into formation to fight off the ambush. But the grassland and thin bush remained silent. No attack came. Nothing happened. They reconnoitred; there was no sign of the enemy. Had the Simbas planted the mines then made off without following up? It did not make sense.

Gradually the shaken group, ears still ringing, began to relax slightly. But they were still in deep trouble. Five Commando was desperately short of radio equipment; they had nothing with them. Here were three men desperately needing medical attention and the entire group needing rescue before nightfall. They were eight miles from Baraka. There was nothing for it but to leg it back and get reinforcements. Don't order anything you would not be prepared to do yourself. Duffy ordered Cummings to join him in a jog-trot along the track back to Baraka; the rest to fan out in a defensive disposition until help arrived. Cummings was carrying his

FN semi-automatic rifle, Duffy the side-arm of an officer. It was a pitiful defence against a possible ambush, but they stumbled on making slow progress in the soft, exhausting sand. Soon Cummings began to lag badly behind.

Then a rhythmic squeaking was heard and an ancient African man hove into view riding a Raleigh bicycle with balloon tyres, that seemed to ride the soft sand of the track like a camel. Duffy, a Swahili speaker, stopped him and entered negotiations. The old man agreed that Duffy could borrow his bicycle to ride back to Baraka for help, but insisted he should be allowed to run alongside to take ownership again. But when Duffy mounted the Raleigh and tried to pedal through the soft sand, he found he lacked the skills. He made no headway at all. So he struck another deal with the old man. He gave him a note to the officer commanding at Baraka. The old African fellow glided away across the sand on his Raleigh, as if in his natural element, and eventually a jeep appeared from Baraka. The casualties were evacuated, the mined truck was eventually taken in tow (the rear axle and wheels were found lying 100 yards away from the point of detonation); alternative arrangements were made to get the ammunition to Firizi and the rest of the party were taken back to Baraka.

It had been an unnerving incident that raised all kinds of questions. Why had the Simba laid landmines but not followed up with an ambush? It did not make sense. The answer could lie in the brutish nature of the Congo conflict; in the character of some of the mercenaries who had enlisted and revelled in that brutishness. It might have had nothing to do with the Simba at all.

When the Armee National Congolaise sappers had arrived at the jetty to set up their landmine sweep, one of them failed to salute Colonel John Peters, officer commanding, when he went down to meet them. Reprimanded, this soldier showed a truculence that enraged Peters, who ordered him to be flung into the cells. There he was systematically beaten with hosepipes and knuckledusters by Five Commando men from the backstreets of Johannesburg (it is not known whether Peters was aware of this), some of whom invited Duffy to join them in the fun. Duffy recoiled from it and was appalled that low-life hoodlums should be allowed licence of this sort.

He believes the landmine that had blown up his scout vehicle – and killed one of his men – could well have been placed by the Congolese sappers themselves in retaliation for what had been done to their comrade by Five Commando men. The landmine had been planted not far from the sappers' camp. Duffy suspected it from the start but dared not breathe a word of it. Given the character of so many of the mercenaries, officers included, it could have led to violent reprisals, fighting between two forces that were supposed to be on the same side. To this day, Duffy is uncertain of the truth of the matter, but the conjecture of itself captures the essential ugliness and the moral ambivalence, at best, of a mercenary operation. Some might go in with the highest motives of preserving peace and stability; out of a spirit of adventure. Others without doubt range in motivation from a desire to plunder to whatever it is that propels the psychopath.

KEEP THE DEPOSIT!

If life was tough and spasmodically terrifying in the eastern Congo, furlough time between contracts was celebrated to excess. The Five Commando men were in town – in Duffy's case Durban – with money in their pockets and ready to whoop it up. Duffy generally found himself in the company of Jim Hayden, a tall Englishman of distinguished looks and manner, and Mike Clynch, a tough little Australian. They generally dossed on the floor of a flat in the Point area, belonging to a waitress named Tina, with whom the relationship of all three was strictly platonic, and they did not stint themselves when it came to entertainment. Only the best would suffice.

The July Handicap was approaching. The Durban July, at Greyville, is South Africa's premier horserace, a social and fashion high point and pinnacle of Durban's July season, which is in the depth of the sub-tropical Natal winter, when the skies are blue and cloudless and the air has the cool crispness of champagne. The threesome decided the July was where they were going to cut a dash. Plans formulated. They would hire morning suits for the occasion, tailcoats and top hats. That would be the way to impress.

The focus of the threesome had meanwhile gravitated slightly to Pietermaritzburg, the gracious, red-brick Victorian capital of the province, some sixty miles inland and sitting at an altitude of about two thousand feet. Duffy was in a dalliance with a winsome student on the Pietermaritzburg campus of the University of Natal, which had drawn them into contact with a different circle. Among these were three nurses at Grey's Hospital who owned a bicycle built for three – an extra-elongated tandem taking one more rider. It was decided that this would be the ideal vehicle on which to arrive at the Durban July in top hats and tails. This would cut a dash in no uncertain terms. The girls agreed to lend it for the purpose.

But to successfully ride such a bicycle is another matter. It is long and unwieldy and to get the three riders to behave in unison when it came to leaning and so forth does not come naturally. Practice is required. Duffy, Hayden and Clynch set about practising on the streets of Pietermaritzburg which, though relatively quiet, do have some abrupt corners and downward descents. They found it awkward. Apart from anything else the lead rider, who steered the contraption and was otherwise in charge, had no control over the brakes because the distance between the front handlebars and the rear wheel was too great for a brake cable to operate effectively. The brakes were therefore on the handlebars of the third rider, the man in the rear, who was not in the best position to see approaching danger. Orders to brake had to be relayed to him, rather as the commands are given on a ship's bridge. It was not ideal in terms of the highway code.

One morning they were pedalling down a street in the central business district, getting their co-ordination and balance together pretty well, when suddenly the surface fell away into a steep descent and they involuntarily picked up speed. Then a severe left-hand corner rushed at them. Duffy, as lead rider, was yelling for the brakes. As they rushed into the bend they were in the middle of the road – and coming towards them, also in the middle of the road, was a small lorry. The three leaned every which way as Duffy tried evasive action. Somehow they missed the lorry but they were totally out of control and tumbled into one of those deep, brick-lined gutters that line the older streets of Pietermaritzburg, having at one time served as irrigation canals. They crashed in a tangle, the bicycle-built-for-three a mangled wreck (it had to be rebuilt completely at their expense) though they escaped physically unscathed apart from bumps, bruises and abrasions. This was no way to cut a dash at the Durban July, which was by now only a matter of days away.

They whistled up Plan B. They would instead go to Greyville racecourse in Duffy's open 1929 Chevrolet. It might be more elegant after all. They hired the morning suits at Woolfsons' Outfitters and the shop assistant taking their measurements tittered at the good humour of Clynch as he wondered whether there would be room under the jacket for his shoulder holster. July Day – always the first Saturday in July – dawned bright and clear, as it always did, and they broke open a bottle of champagne as they dressed in Tina's flat. Then they discovered an omission. They had hired tailcoats, trousers, top hats, gloves and shoes – but they had no black socks. It would not do to spoil the effect with fluorescent purple or something like that. They considered. Then the solution dawned. They smeared their ankles with black boot polish and wore no socks at all. Thus attired in morning suits and toppers, but sans socks, they were ready to cut a dash. They finished the second bottle of champagne and set off in the 1929 Chevrolet.

"There's a bottle store," said Hayden.

"Quite right. Why are we going past?" said Clynch.

Duffy stopped and they went inside and bought a few more bottles of champagne.

The main gate at Greyville racecourse was thronged with people, the road outside choked with traffic. Duffy parked with skill on a yellow line.

"You can't park here!" The policeman was outraged.

"Why not?"

"It's a yellow line. You'll get a ticket!"

The patrician Hayden entered the conversation.

"For how much?"

"Fifty rands." (Which was a tidy sum in the 1960s).

Hayden roared with laughter and graciously waved his top hat. "Oh, we can easily afford that, my good man."

"You'll get towed away!"

At which Duffy decided they had better move on. Cars were parked all the way along the streets. But they came to a building site where nobody could park because the builder had placed barrels and planks at the roadside where his vehicles came in and out during the week. These were easily removed. Duffy drove in and parked on the building site and the barrels and planks were put back. They had their own personal parking, a short walk from the main gate. Cheers came from above where people at the back of one of the Greyville grandstands had been observing the manoeuvre. Hayden turned and graciously bowed, doffing his top hat. Then he turned again, slammed shut the car door and strode off with aplomb.

Then a blood-curdling r-r-r-rip! One of his coat tails had caught in the car door. His hired tailcoat had ripped right up to the neck.

Nothing daunted, they strode into the Greyville crowd, doffing their top hats and bowing to anyone who caught their eye, Hayden not quite as immaculate as he could have been but polished nevertheless. They found a spot in one of the observation lounges and proceeded to place bets and drink champagne. They cheered every result as if they had won, whatever happened. When you celebrate every race in a 12-race meeting, a head of steam builds up. Eventually they moved on to mingle with the crowd, then found themselves in another bar under the main grandstand. Here matters turned awkward. Loutish elements showed disdain for their top hats, which were placed on the bar counter, and mocked their apparel generally. Somebody poured beer into one of the hats; somebody else used one as an ashtray and caused a small fire which had to be extinguished with more beer. The men of Five Commando did not take kindly to provocation of this sort and a melee ensured, during which somebody jumped on one of the top hats, squashing it flat as a pancake. But Five Commando could handle themselves in any bar fight and eventually prevailed. But one top hat was flattened, one was scorched and the other had disappeared altogether. The gloves of all three were smeared with the blood of their opponents. Hayden's tailcoat was ripped from top to bottom.

They went into Woolfsons' next day with everything packed back into the boxes. Duffy waited outside with engine running. Clynch went inside with the hired gear and thrust it at the first shop assistant he saw.

"Here's our stuff. You can keep the deposit!" Then he was gone.

***

Duffy, Hayden and Clynch were lounging about Tina's flat. Hayden was reading the newspaper. Then suddenly he was on his feet, electrified.

"Hey, look at this job! This is for us!"

The advertisement was for crew to collect a yacht in Italy and take it down the Suez Canal, all the way to Cape Town. The newspaper passed from one to the others. They were infused with excitement. Replies should be to a post office box number in Cape Town or to a street address.

"They'll stampede for this job," said Clynch. "How do we get in first?"

There was no telephone number given, just the post office box number and the street address. The only way was to get down there and pitch. But it had to be done fast. Dozens of people would be applying. They telephoned airline bookings. Nothing to Cape Town was available that evening. Driving in spells it was possible to get from Durban to Cape Town virtually overnight if there was no stopping. It was worth a chance. Next stop was a car hire firm where they hired a gleaming Dodge Valiant for a week. Then back to Tina's to pick up their gear.

Tina was reading the newspaper. "Fellows, I don't want to spoil your fun," she said. "But have you read this ad properly?"

They checked again. It was for people who would pay for the pleasure of crewing a yacht from Italy to Cape Town via the Suez Canal. It was not a job offer at all. Absolute deflation. And they had hired a Dodge Valiant for the week. They might as well make the best of it. Girls were very impressed by the gleaming beast.

On the back seat they found a chauffeur's cap. Clynch and Hayden developed a system. One would take the wheel wearing the chauffeur's cap and the other would recline in the back seat giving the eye to girls on the beachfront and elsewhere. Then they would exchange positions. It amused them and they did get to pick up quite a few girls. Duffy was not a participant at this stage because he was still amorously involved in Pietermaritzburg, where he had also joined a karate dojo.

Then came a time when a decision had to be made. Duffy and his girl were going to a party in Pietermaritzburg that promised to be a whingdinger. Hayden and Clynch were both invited. Hayden wanted to accept but Clynch had arranged a rendezvous in Durban that very night with girls they had been taking out for weeks and had already scored with. A bird in the hand, Clynch argued. But Hayden disagreed. Fresh pastures, he argued. They argued and argued but could not agree.

Eventually, sitting in a small bar just off the beachfront, they agreed how to decide the matter. It was the kind of thing that happens in forlorn messes deep in the Congo. They would match each other drink for drink. The one who was left standing would decide whether they stayed in Durban that night or went to Pietermaritzburg. The drinks came in steady succession and were disposed of. It was already evening by the time Clynch slumped senseless on the bar counter and Hayden weaved his way to the Valiant, started it and pointed it in the direction of Pietermaritzburg.

He was about a third of the way there, on the escarpment climbing to the interior at a place called Drummond, that he got into an inexplicable wobble and wrapped the Valiant around a roadside telephone pole. It was already dark as he climbed out of the wreckage and stood there swaying. Next thing a police van had pulled up and a young constable was speaking to him.

"What happened, man?"

"It's a crisis," said Hayden in his most clipped upper-crust tones. "I'm a surgeon at Grey's Hospital in Pietermaritzburg. I'm on my way to perform an emergency operation. Now the patient may die."

"My magtig!" Many people have an instinctive deference to the patrician Englishman. This Afrikaner police constable was among them. "I'll see what I can do."

Drummond is on the main railway line from Durban to Johannesburg. Mainline trains do not stop at the small station, but that night one did. The express train to Johannesburg was stopped as an emergency and the "doctor" was helped aboard with the good wishes of the police and all concerned. An air of distinction and breeding trumped such trivialities as liquor fumes.

"Can I get you some coffee, Doctor?" asked the steward.

"No thanks. You can get me a drink."

Later that evening Hayden stumbled into the party in Pietermaritzburg, having taken a taxi from the station (which was a scheduled stop). Then he passed out before he could complete telling his story. Next morning he telephoned the car hire firm in Durban.

"You'll find your Valiant parked against a telephone pole near Drummond station. Keep the deposit!"

***

It was another furlough after yet another contract in the Congo. Hayden and Clynch were this time together in England, just the two of them. What could provide the greatest contrast to the privations of constant patrols and skirmishes in equatorial Africa? They decided a narrowboat on the canals would be just the thing. The narrowboats took one through the idyllic English countryside at a sedate pace. Nobody was about to spring an ambush. The water contained no crocodiles or hippo. It was summer, the countryside drifted by: farms, copses, fields of cows and sheep; fields of grain. A constant choice showed itself of the most charming waterside pubs. This was indeed a holiday, a relaxation.

The first day out they tied up at a jetty at lunch time and made their way to a pub that belonged in a picture postcard. They drank pints of beer. They ate lunch. They played darts. They fondled the dogs. They chatted to the locals and to the other narrowboat people who would, like themselves, spend the night on the water in their craft. They flirted with the girls with great gallantry though no serious intent. This was relaxation, this was the life.

That evening they made their way down the jetty. Their narrowboat was gone. Horrors! Then they spotted the painter that had held it tied up. It led directly through the water to a spot under a nearby humped-back stone bridge. While they were making merry in the pub, the water level had dropped with the tide. The narrowboat had drifted under the bridge. Then, while they were still making merry, the tide had come in again. The boat became trapped under the bridge, the mast pushed through its planking and it then sank like a stone and was suspended there under two fathoms of water.

They went back to the pub and telephoned the narrowboat hire company. "Your boat is tied up outside the King's Arms. Keep the deposit!"

***

Not many members of Five Commando could claim parachutist qualifications. It was on one of those furloughs when Duffy, still in dalliance in Pietermaritzburg and still engrossed in karate, achieved that distinction. Some of the members of his Pietermaritzburg dojo were also members of the Pietermaritzburg Skydiving Club based at Oribi airport, outside the city, which was the first such club ever to have been formed in the British Commonwealth. In the pub one evening they were joshing as to the rival merits of karate and parachuting as disciplines, tests of skill and nerve and so forth. The parachutists – who had experienced both – insisted that parachuting was the superior sport. Duffy said it was nothing but the law of gravity, while karate demanded skill, balance and an attitude of mind. One thing led to another and a wager was struck. Duffy would jump next morning at Oribi.

He arrived very hung over, wearing his Five Commando combat boots. The office-bearers at the parachute club were dubious. A novice could not be allowed to jump without going through the training, learning how to roll on impact and so forth. Duffy argued that he had been jumping and rolling on impact from moving vehicles in the Congo for months now. He was superbly fit, both from the military service and his karate training.

The skydiving club was long-established, as mentioned, but it had just moved into new premises and was desperately raising funds. Individuals were encouraged to "buy" bricks on the wall above the bar counter, for a fairly hefty donation, and their name would remain there in perpetuity. Duffy offered to buy a brick. That clinched it. Next thing he was in a Piper Cub, spiralling up over Oribi and the despatcher was telling him at the open door that when he tapped him twice on the helmet he should go. The static line would do the rest.

It went perfectly. There was no crosswind. Duffy did a near spot-on landing on the aerodrome and rolled as he hit ground as if he were a veteran, to cheers from almost the entire karate club who had turned out to watch. This was to create tensions with the owner of the dojo because half his members switched their allegiance to parachuting instead of karate, but Duffy never was tempted to do the same. Karate was to become a dominant theme in his life. But his name is still on that brick in the Pietermaritzburg Parachute Club.

LONGJOHNS

The campaign in the eastern Congo could sometimes take a strange turn. Duffy had risen to the rank of captain and was actually in command at Baraka, the rest of 5 Commando having moved on, when he took a decision described by his Scots sergeant-major as a "gr-r-e-e-e-t mistake", which was to have unexpected ramifications. Intelligence told them a village about two days' march away in the mountains had been heavily infiltrated by Simbas. Five Commando's tactic was to act on such information right away, attack the insurgents, taking them by surprise before they could start intimidating the local populace. He took a platoon of about 20 with him, reached the locality after dark and was able to view the village through binoculars at first light. Nobody was stirring at that stage but the intelligence was highly credible. It was a large village and would require an assault of sharp shock and force if it were to be subdued. The platoon moved in and opened up, raking the mud walls with automatic fire. The fate of those inside did not bear thinking of.

This was the moment of queasiness when it could be revealed that their intelligence was wrong, the place was occupied only by civilians. But two figures came out of the nearest doorway with AK-47s in a state of sheer bewilderment, not returning a shot as they were gunned down. Then others, they too meeting the same fate. Surprise was total. The platoon moved from door to door, throwing in grenades where nobody emerged. Suddenly women and children were there in the confusion, running and wailing, and the attackers did their best to let them go without harm. But overall it was the tragic, bloody mess of all such attacks. Duffy's group moved through the entire village. The Simba had been there in strength. Those that were not lying dead in the dust had presumably managed to escape into the surrounding bush. It was always the way with such incidents. Male villagers had their hands in the air, protesting their innocence. The place was shrill with lamentation.

Where was the Simba arms store? Such a large group must have had an armoury of sorts. They searched, hut to hut, then eventually came to a building that appeared to be not a dwelling but some kind of store. Kicking down the door, they found what they were after: a stockpile of AK-47s and crates of ammunition, mines and other materiel. Clearly, this had been a major Simba base. It was dark in there and Duffy flashed a torch about the place. Suddenly he sensed as much as heard a stirring. Then the torchlight picked out the whites of a pair of staring eyes. The muzzles of several FN rifles swung toward them. A figure was crouching on the floor, terrified. Duffy spokes to him in Swahili. "Come forward slowly. Hands in the air." To his astonishment, the stirring became general. A whole lot of figures were coming toward him slowly, hands in the air, absolutely unmenacing.

Outside in the sunlight, there were 14 of them. They were Simbas. Some had been guarding the arms store, others had taken refuge with them when the firing broke out. Not one had attempted to take and load an AK-47. They were shocked and stunned and shivered as they awaited their fate.

Duffy ascertained who the leader was. He had him sat down under a tree and started interrogating in Swahili. He got his name, home district and home village; where he had been recruited by the Simba, where he had received training. He did the same with a few of the others. And he soon came to the conclusion that these Simba knew absolutely nothing about the struggle they were involved in, who they were fighting against or why. All they could do was half-heartedly parrot some revolutionary jargon they had been taught. They seemed to have no idea that the Congo was actually under the rule of an African leader. And they were totally demoralised.

He considered. This was an unusual situation. The Simba who were not killed in a contact invariably fled the scene. To have prisoners on one's hands was something entirely new. Duffy ordered his group – who had suffered zero casualties – to march them back to Baraka, hands bound. Once arrived there, they were given food and water and put under close guard. He still did not know what to do with them. Some of the men had their own suggestions as to what should be done, but he ignored them. He planned an experiment in psychology.

The 5 Commando camp at Baraka had beside it a football pitch, used by the local children. It was also an airdrop point for overseas charities. Every few weeks a chartered Dakota would fly over and drop out huge bales of clothing and bedding for the succour of the suffering people of the Congo. The bales were bound in steel strips, and these would somehow hold as the cargo was dead-dropped onto the ground from hundreds of feet, bouncing and rolling until they came to rest. The aircrew were pretty accurate in their bombing; they had been doing it in various parts of the Congo.

The Congo and the plight of its people had touched the conscience of the world, the Western democracies especially. Whether the content of the bales of emergency aid dropped was appropriate to the people's needs was another matter. They included such items as moleskin trousers and tweed jackets, not exactly in demand in equatorial Africa. They also included longjohns, those full-length white flannel underpants that reach right down to the ankles, so comforting in a London winter.

Duffy outlined his plan to his officers and NCOs. "Ye're mad, sir!" exclaimed the Scots sergeant-major. "Ye're making a gre-e-e-t mistake!" But Duffy was insistent. The fourteen prisoners would be allowed to wash and brush up on the edge of the lake. Then each would be issued with a pair of longjohns and a carton of cigarettes from the Commando's stores. Then – and this is what really raised the ire of the sergeant-major – each would have his AK-47 returned to him, properly cleaned and with a clip of five rounds of ammunition. This was partly for his self-protection in the bush, partly so he could shoot for the pot but mainly to show good faith. The war was over, Duffy told them. They must return to their people and spread the message.

The Simbas paused briefly for photographs in their new longjohns, then took off smartly into the bush, watched by the scandalized sergeant-major and those who thought like him. He posted extra sentries that night. They would be back, he was certain.

It was a few days before the Simbas were back, but it was not the same ones. These were a group of about 20, there to surrender and claim their longjohns and cigarettes. It started to snowball. A week later, 300 had pitched up at Baraka. Five Commando's cigarette stocks ran low. They ran out of longjohns and had to make do with moleskin trousers and tweed jackets, just the thing for the Congo. But the rebellion was over in that region. The Peace of the Longjohns was to hold.

***

Duffy was to serve three contracts with Five Commando. It was dangerous and exhausting work, monotony alternating with adrenalin rushes. It was also, in the very nature of war, pretty ghastly. They were almost constantly out in the bush, often on low rations. Every contract ended with a period of home leave, and then the enjoyment was riotous. But back in the Congo there was no respite.

It could perhaps have continued indefinitely. The Congo today, almost fifty years later, is as convulsed with violence and brutality as it ever was, the eastern regions in particular, where there is a strong input of instability from Rwanda, Burundi and Uganda. The Tutu-Hutsi animosity of those countries is played out in the Congo as well.

However, Five Commando's operation came to an abrupt end as Duffy was approaching the closure of his third contract. It was caused by Congolese internal politics, a sudden cooling between President Mobutu and the CIA and a fear on his part (possibly well justified) that foreign mercenaries might well be used to remove him. Mobutu unilaterally cancelled his contract with Five Commando and, after initial hesitation, paid them out in full, at which they flew back to South Africa and thence to whichever part of the world they came from.

The same thing happened to Six Commando, under Colonel Jean Schramme, though not as smoothly. Six Commando was much closer integrated with the Congolese government than Five Commando had ever been; many of its officers, Schramme included, were Belgians. Six Commando had linked up with Katangese gendarmes – the best-trained, best-disciplined and most potent indigenous force in the Congo – and were refusing to disperse or disarm until they were paid. Mutiny seemed to be brewing until at last Six Commando were paid and allowed to embark on a lake steamer, fully armed, for a landfall in Tanganyika, from where they dispersed.

But the unfortunate Katangese were left stranded and were eventually machinegunned in an act of utter treachery by troops of the Armee National Congolaise as they washed at the lakeside. Many escaped the massacre and fled into Angola, where they regrouped, along with their families, and remained in a state of armed readiness, nurturing an abiding hatred of Mobutu and all he stood for. When the Portuguese decolonised in Angola, the

Katangese sided with the Marxist MPLA movement, not out of any kind of ideological conviction but because Mobutu was with the CIA again and against the MPLA. In the ensuing civil war, they were a useful adjunct to the MPLA/Soviet/Cuban effort.

However, as noted, Duffy was not a political animal. For him a chapter had closed and it was time to look around for fresh adventure.

JAPAN

Duffy had flung himself with enthusiasm into karate of the shukokai style, which was being taught at a dojo in Pietermaritzburg by a Japanese master named Kimaru. He went to the dojo every day, training hard to hone his fitness and perfect his technique. Then Kimaru left to return to Japan and the group in Pietermaritzburg who had attached themselves to him felt a vacuum. Duffy and four others, including Des Botes, owner of the dojo, decided they had best follow Kimaru to Japan and train further. It had long been Duffy's ambition to visit the Far East and he was totally captured by karate – its strict yet generous ethos and its combativeness. In 1988 the five sailed from Durban in the Tegelberg, an ancient P&O liner carrying passengers from South America to Japan.

It was very much a low-budget venture. They shared a cramped cabin in the bowels of the ship, just above the propeller shaft. They would eat with the crew. This would be anything but a luxury cruise. They were allowed nowhere near the first and second class decks. But their spirits were high and were lifted further when Marion – Duffy's girlfriend from the Pietermaritzburg campus of the university – arrived to see them off with a novelty gift: a giant, five-gallon plastic bottle which she had filled with chianti wine. They had guessed (correctly as it turned out) that the fare of the crew would not be much to their taste so they had smuggled aboard as much tinned food as they could, as well as a small primus stove. They would cook illegally in their cabin.

One problem: they had neglected to bring with them a tin opener or a cooking pot. They were able to open the tins with knives but cooking was a problem until they discovered that the ship's purser, who was also quartered far below decks, had the habit of leaving a tin shaving mug outside his cabin door every morning. They would take the mug each day, clean it, cook in it, then clean it again and put it back for collection. This went on for the entire voyage without their being detected. (They counted themselves fortunate that it was a shaving mug and not any other domestic utensil).

But the dozens of children quartered nearby could not be fooled. These were Japanese children who had been brought up in Brazil and spoke nothing but Portuguese and were going to Japan to meet their grandparents. They soon smelled the food cooking and would besiege the Duffy group's cabin, sharing the fun and a little of the food as well. They never did let on to their elders.

The Tegelberg docked at Singapore and the five went ashore to sample the delights of the Orient, not least the massage. At Hong-Kong it was much the same except that here they met up with a Chinese who was courtesy driver at one the swish hotels. This man took them on a tour of the parts of Hong-Kong not seen by tourists, where the liquor was absurdly cheap and where the ordinary folk let their hair down. It was the time of the limbo dancing craze and in one night spot Duffy managed to split his trousers doing it. Their new companion took them to a tailor's shop for the trousers to be repaired and Duffy carried on the spree wearing some kind of kimono. They ended up on a sampan in the harbour drinking beer that had a dragon on the bottle's label plus various other concoctions.

Next day all five felt like death but Duffy had to go ashore to collect his trousers before the ship sailed. He took a walla-walla boat (so named for the noise the exhaust makes as it goes through the wavelets) and stepped ashore. But everything looked unfamiliar in the light of day and he struggled at first to find the tailor's shop. Sailing time was almost there by the time he found the tailor's, paid for the repairs and took another walla-walla boat.

Duffy maintained his record in unorthodox boarding of passenger liners. Tegelberg had already started moving, though very slowly, as the walla-walla boat approached. The gangplank had not yet been drawn in and was still down the ship's side. But its first rungs were still high above the walla-walla boat as it drew alongside. To cheers from his karate companions who were watching anxiously from the rail, Duffy managed to leap high enough to grab the gangplank then haul himself up and make his way on board. It had been a close thing. He would otherwise have found himself stranded in Hong-Kong with no passport, no money and no return ticket. His career would doubtless have taken a course other than the pursuit of karate.

The voyage was otherwise uneventful and soon enough they docked at Kobe, a Japanese town about 25 minutes away by bullet train from Osaka, where Kimaru had his dojo. Initially they dossed at the dojo, washing the floors and cleaning up generally every morning before the day's training began, but then they moved into lodgings – an astonishingly flimsy little house (like most Japanese dwellings) set against the mountainside with the rock face as one of the walls, down which water streamed when the rains came. But it was near the dojo and convenient. This was to be Duffy's home and lifestyle for the next two years. His companions from Pietermaritzburg drifted home in the weeks and months ahead but he stayed put. He was enthused with karate, for which he showed great aptitude, and pursued it single-mindedly. He also picked up the Japanese language.

He trained hard and was to achieve Third Dan level. He and Kimaru competed or put on shukokai exhibitions at clubs and universities at various centres in Japan, travelling extensively. In exhibitions, Duffy always went into the ring with the master, Kimaru, which gained him extra experience and expertise and also made him a well-known figure in various centres. Kimaru also set about producing an illustrated manual on shokukai, in English, Duffy supplying the text and posing with Kimaru for photographs of the different manoeuvres. This too was to give his karate an extra edge, something beyond his Third Dan level.

At virtually every centre a sprinkling of westerners was to be found, like Duffy there to learn karate but eager also to socialise with their own kind. It was through these that Duffy was to launch into an occupation in parallel with karate – teaching English to the Japanese. He was dubious when the idea was first put to him by a large, genial Cockney he had encountered at one of the karate meetings. What did he know about English, let alone teaching it?

But it turned out to be nothing like the study of the English classics at Gordonstoun, as he discovered when the Cockney invited him to attend one of his own classes to see what went on.

"Wotcher, Cock!" he greeted them as he strode into the classroom.

"Wotcher, Cock!" the Japanese students solemnly chorused back at him.

Duffy decided this was too good to miss. He advertised and very soon had 20 or so Japanese girls enrolled for his own classes, held at his lodgings. They were keen as mustard to learn English and fascinated by westerners. They were also, he was discover, eager for extra-mural amorous activity if he should show the inclination but (with one notable exception) he held back from such complications. He still went to the karate dojo every day but twice a week took an English class at his lodgings; and very merry classes they were too, where the Japanese girls had their English vocabulary enriched with choice bits of Scots dialect. It was a lot of fun and also a source of significant income. These were working girls, willing to pay to improve their employability by speaking English.

Duffy was to develop a great respect for the Japanese and their culture, so vividly embodied in the ethos of karate. They were a people of a great underlying seriousness. They considered their words and actions carefully, chose the right phrases, concerned never to cause the other party to lose face, a calamity in Japanese culture. They were free of sexual inhibition – not obsessed by it but accepting of it. A visit to a bath-house automatically involved sexual frolicking, the criterion being mutual enjoyment, nothing more. Yet there could be surprises.

One of Duffy's western acquaintances, a Canadian named Bert, was standing in the street one day when an old Japanese woman came pedalling along on her bicycle. She hailed him in reasonably good English and struck up a conversation. She wanted to introduce him to her daughter, she said. She had a beautiful daughter. She wanted to meet a westerner. Bert must come to her house nearby and meet her daughter, she insisted.

Eventually Bert did stroll along with her. They went into a house where he was introduced to an indeed beautiful Japanese girl. Things seemed to be going along swimmingly as she suddenly took him by the hand and led him away. Then, to Bert's bewilderment, he noted that the house seemed to be filling up with men. Almost too late, he realised what was happening. He and the beautiful daughter were about to star in a peephole show. The men had come off the street and paid to watch the performance. He fled through the front door.

During his two years in Japan, Duffy struck up a long-term relationship with only two women, one of them a Korean. But they came to nothing in the end. His status there was strictly transitory. But before he left he developed another sideline, one which was to significantly propel his career for a time. Japan had a burgeoning film industry in the 1960s, which supplied not just the cinemas but television as well. The demand for low-budget material was constant and many scripts required western characters. Through his circle of western expatriates, Duffy made contact with a studio in Osaka, and from then on he was a regular at film shoots, usually in the evenings and often lasting late into the night. He would be collected from home in a chauffeur-driven car and dropped off again when the shoot was finished. Sometimes he would be a stunt man standing in for the regular actor in a fight scene or motorcycle crash scene; sometimes he would simply be an extra; occasionally he would have a small speaking part. But the pay was good and the work appealed to him. So by the time Duffy left Japan he was riding three horses: karate, teaching English and appearing in low-budget films. It made the week a full one.

When he left it was to follow karate. Kimaru wanted to travel to Paris where local dojos wanted exhibitions of shukokai. He wanted his regular exhibition partner, Duffy, to go with him. There were cheaper ways to get to Paris from Japan than flying. They took a ship to the Soviet port of Vladivostok and from there took the Trans-Siberia Express to Moscow; from Moscow, they took the Oriental Express to Paris. They crossed the snowy wastes of Russia, an awe-inspiring experience in itself – then crossed the sparse expanses of Eastern Europe to reach the glittering jewel of Paris. It was the very depth of the Cold War. During his brief sojourn in Moscow, Duffy was struck by the numbers of people everywhere, women as well as men, who were in uniform. Much the same was true of the other Warsaw Pact countries. Arrived in Paris (and then later in Britain) he encountered for the first time the western hippy generation: the unkept beards and hair, the filthy clothing, the scruffiness and the sheer vacancy of the individuals involved. It left him with a sense of deep unease compared with the order, discipline and purpose he had just left behind in the Eastern bloc. But Duffy had never been a political animal. He turned his attention to the task in hand, which was the promotion of shukokai in Paris and anywhere else in Europe that might show an interest.

GOING IRISH

Arrived in Paris, Duffy, Kimaru and the rest of the group made contact with Mandu, owner of a long-established dojo in the city and a man of great sophistication and influence who had lived in France a long time and had a French wife. He had close contact with the French special forces and very soon the group would be demonstrating the shukokai style to special forces exponents of unarmed combat, using a special gymnasium in the vaults beneath the French parliament. Mandu had them placed in accommodation and they saw as much as they could of the great city and its restaurant and night life as their schedule at the dojo and elsewhere allowed. For the next few months they demonstrated shukokai to various karate groups from elsewhere in Europe, including one from Norway. These invited Duffy to travel back to Oslo with them to show the style to other members of their association so they could decide if they also wanted to make the trip to Paris to learn. This he did, the group making the trip overland by car, and it paid off because next the Norwegians sent another strong group to Mandu's dojo to learn.

Duffy had been away from Britain in Africa and the Orient for 24 years by this time. Now he was just across the water from his family and he decided to make a trip to Elgin to visit. Typically, he planned to drop in unannounced. But he was the one to be surprised. When he got to Elgin his parents were not in residence at their home outside the town. Tenants were there instead. Asking around, he discovered that they had relocated to a placed named Newtownmountkennedy, just south of Dublin, in Ireland. He obtained a telephone number for them and caught a flight to Dublin.

His appearance had changed considerably since leaving Japan, let alone since he had last been in Britain. He had grown a full beard. He had acquired a Russian fur hat and Russian top boots designed for snow. He complemented this with a Norwegian sweater of raw wool and a pair of cavalry-style blue trousers. Thus kitted out, he began to explore Dublin as a preliminary to making contact with his parents and in a pub one afternoon he encountered a kindred spirit named McGurk, who helped him explore the city in fine style. They roistered together for a week before Duffy eventually got around to telephoning. Duffy had by now developed a fair imitation of McGurk's Irish brogue.

The telephone was answered by Duffy's stepfather, Sassoon. Duffy launched into a torrent of stage Irish. "Ah, good afternoon to yez, Oi've been doin' some work on de rigs in Poland and Oi met your son, Peter Duffy, and he gave me someting and asked if Oi could pass it on tae yez."

"Oh yes?"

"If you can just give me your address Oi'll bring it round tomorrow, to be sure, to be sure."

Sassoon was not giving away his whereabouts. "That's very kind of you. I think it better if we meet at the Grafton Hotel, in town." They set up a time for next day.

The Grafton was a genteel place, the clientele in hacking jackets, the staff floating discreetly about in dress suits. Duffy spotted his stepfather sitting alone in a lounge chair. He bore down on him. Sassoon flinched at the fur cap, beard, sweater, cavalry trousers and boots.

"Mr Sassoon I do believe, ah to be sure, to be sure. McGurk is de name."

"Er, how do you do?"

"Foine tank you, foine!" He took a seat. A waiter was hovering.

"Er, can I get you anything?"

"Tank you, a Guinness would go down foine! First today, 'tis a shame, 'tis a shame!"

"A pint of Guinness please. I'll have a coffee."

Duffy then launched into another torrent of stage Irish. He was enjoying himself hugely. He was beginning to explain how he had met Peter while working on some kind of oil rig when the waiter returned with the order. Duffy took a healthy swig.

"Cheers! Like de missionaries say, may de skin of your bum never cover a drum!"

But Sassoon was staring into his face.

"My God, boy! It's you!" You can put on a fur cap and grow a beard but you cannot disguise your eyes. The old boy had cottoned on. He turned back to the waiter. "Bring me a large whiskey!"

And in this way Duffy returned briefly for a time to the bosom of his family. He went back to the new family home in Ireland to meet his mother – who had been forewarned by Sassoon by telephone – and he was to meet up again with his elder brother who was working in Ireland. His parents kept quiet about his presence, so he was again able to put on the McGurk impersonation when he met up with him. The reunion was tumultuous.

Duffy also started looking about for film work, for which he had acquired a taste in Japan. He made inquiries which led him to Ardmore Studios, located at Bray, in Dublin, and work as a stunt extra doubling for the stars gradually developed into slightly more substantial roles, sometimes even speaking roles. His finest moment was when he was cast as a Gestapo officer interrogating a captured British woman agent, a stunningly beautiful Irish actress. The script required him to roughly rip off her blouse as she sat bound to a chair, then feign a stubbing of a cigarette on the region above her breasts. Duffy seized the blouse and ripped. But unfortunately he had also grabbed the lady's bra underneath and the whole lot came away. Audiences about the world would have paid anything to see her pneumatic properties bouncing free in close proximity, as Duffy did, but alas the cameras stopped whirring.

Duffy was enjoying himself greatly. He was to spend another two years in Ireland working at the film studio. Gradually his direct involvement in karate diminished, though he was involved in a championship contest in London, along with his shukokai comrades from Paris. At that meeting he knocked out a gigantic German opponent who had otherwise been wreaking havoc and perhaps as a result of that he was chosen for the British team that went to the world championships in Yugoslavia, where he enjoyed success. But karate was not big in Ireland and his involvement abated.

Then came the turn of events that took him back to Africa. Ardmore Studios travelled to South-West Africa – then still a United Nations mandate administered by South Africa – to make *Creatures That The World Forgot*, a horror film starring Australian Tony Bonner, Irishman Sean O'Shaughnessy and Norwegian pin-up of the day, Julie Edge. It was a strong cast. Duffy was there as a stuntman stand-in for Bonner as well as extra. But the film was one of the genre appreciated best by the bingo hall ladies with their hair in curlers and a bag of bullseyes. The London critics called it "the film the world should forget" and, sure enough, it soon did.

But Duffy was back in Africa, experiencing again its qualities of light, its cadences, its sights and sounds. He was in contact again with people such as Barney Carey, who he had been with in Tanganyika and the Congo. There was good money to be made taking heavy trucks along the "hell run" from Rhodesia to Mozambique, where the giant Cahora Bassa dam was being built on the Zambesi and where a guerrilla insurgency against the colonial Portuguese was starting to intensify. This sounded like the old life. When the film set struck camp, he headed for Johannesburg.

Duffy in his heyday

Duffy as a Nazi officer ... on a film set in Ireland

Swastika armband ... still on film set

The Frothblowers' captured weaponry on display

South African special forces guard the arrested Frothblowers in an army truck at Durban international airport

The hijacked Boeing at Durban international airport

Duffy hams it up on the Durban beachfront with Air India cabin crew ... some years later

Duffy with an Air India officer after the first scheduled landing at Durban international airport

How cartoonist Jock Leyden saw Duffy's escapades in Africa

Seychelles scene ... a small hotel

Seychellois crowds demonstrate at the trial in Victoria of the captured
Frothblowers advance party

THE HELL RUN

Stories had been filtering through about problems the Portuguese were having with Frelimo guerrilla attacks on the trucks supplying material to the giant Cahora Bassa dam project on the Zambesi, in Mozambique; also of attacks on workers at the dam site itself. Would this not be an opportunity for the men of the now disbanded 5 Commando? Duffy, Barney Carey and a few others put together a proposal for a mercenary force to protect the truck convoys, which ran almost daily, via Rhodesia, between the Witwatersrand, South Africa's industrial heartland, and the dam site in Tete province, in Mozambique; possibly also to protect the dam site. Every bit of concrete, every piece of steel and every piece of machinery came by this route. The building of the dam depended on it. The proposal was sent to the Portuguese authorities, who blandly declined the offer, denying that there was any kind of insurgency or emergency at all in Tete. Yet the 5 Commando men met up in the bars of Hillbrow with truckers who were on leave. They spoke of regular ambushes on the long Mozambique leg of the trip; of the heavy lorries being sometimes riddled with bullets and having to travel in huge convoys protected by Portuguese armoured vehicles. Clearly the Portuguese were trying to downplay the insurgency, putting in their own troops to contain it. The 5 Commando men decided an inspection on the spot was needed. Somebody should get a job as a trucker to discover what was really happening.

Duffy happened to have a heavy duty driver's licence. It came about when, shortly after his arrival in Durban from Tanganyika and he was looking about for something to do, the Fire Department advertised for fire engine drivers. Duffy applied and was accepted into the preliminary course, which involved training on heavy duty vehicles and passing the heavy duty driver's test. This he duly did and was issued with a heavy duty licence. He also did things like carry a colleague, fireman's lift, up and down the high ladder from the fire engine, as well as slide down poles and handle high pressure hoses. In ways it was fulfilment of a small boy's dream. But the Durban Corporation had a long and tedious process of finalisation of appointments; appearances before selection panels, endless bureaucratic dawdling. Duffy tired of it all and withdrew, taking up beach photography then nightspot social photography instead, before eventually enlisting for the Congo. But he did have his heavy duty driver's licence.

From a film set in South-West Africa to a transport yard in Alberton, a grimy industrial town south of Johannesburg – Duffy made the transition with aplomb. The transport company had on the road giant 28-wheeler truck and trailer Mercedes Benz rigs, which moved from the Witwatersrand into Rhodesia, stopped overnight at Salisbury, then crossed at Nyamapanda into Mozambique next day, then drove on through the bush on mainly dirt roads to the town of Songo, in Tete province, then the dam site itself, on the

Zambesi. It was wild bush country almost the entire way once the truckers crossed into Mozambique, it was hard and exhausting work (though the Mercedes rigs did at least have power steering) and the truckers fended for themselves and slept at the roadside in lay-bys. The round trip from Alberton to Tete and back usually took about ten days.

Duffy was fortunate in that his first job was to go only as far as Salisbury, as passenger in another lorry, to collect the rig of another driver who had fallen ill and bring it back to Alberton. It gave him the opportunity to learn the routines – gear changing, managing the air brakes and so on – from an old hand, then get a shortish practice run back to base. By the end of this he felt he had mastered the huge, cumbersome vehicle. But very soon he was on his way to Cahora Bassa in earnest and he was to spend the next six months at it. He later switched to another company that also supplied the Zambian Copperbelt, just beneath the Congo border, so the trips became longer and more exhausting (the new company's vehicles were Diamond-Ts, which had no power steering) and Duffy was closer to his old stamping ground.

On the Tete run he saw plenty of evidence of guerilla insurgency: vehicles at the roadside riddled with bullets and burned out. At Cahora Bassa itself he learned first hand of Frelimo attacks on workers, of heavy casualties. But he himself was never to experience direct contact with Frelimo. The area swarmed with Portuguese troops, poorly paid conscripts from distant Portugal who did not have their heart in the struggle and were loathed by the local populace for their habit of forcing themselves sexually on the women. But there were also the Flechas, highly trained, highly committed locally raised soldiers, some Portuguese, some African, some mestico (and some of them turned guerrillas), who were an effective counter-insurgency force, distinctive in their black uniforms.

The transport lorries were supposed to travel in convoy, led by a Portuguese army vehicle, but Duffy preferred to lag behind and avoid the massive dust cloud raised by twenty or thirty vehicles on a dirt road, making conditions gritty and unpleasant. Duffy has always had a penchant for cooking and soon he was indulging it on the road. He developed a method of cooking sausages, chops, vegetables – just about anything – by wrapping them in tinfoil which he then placed in a cage of chicken wire wrapped around the vehicle's exhaust, which rose vertical just beside the cab. Tinned food he also heated that way, bashing the side of the tin to fit against the exhaust. He was enjoying himself, preparing some mouth-watering repasts one would not have thought possible in the African bush. No liquor passed his lips while he was trucking (which was more than could be said of some of his fellow-drivers) and he drove until he was tired, at which he would pull over and sleep in the cab. It was monotonous and tiring work but the money – double-time – was very good indeed and he was prepared to stick it out for a time. Clearly though, there was little scope for a mercenary operation. The Portuguese were doing things their own way and with their own personnel.

Sometimes it rained and this was always problematic because with the load on board the slightest incline could cause difficulties with wheelspin and skidding, even the ultimate horror of sliding off the road altogether. One afternoon in thick bush on the road to

Songo it began to rain. Duffy stopped and considered his options. An incline lay ahead. Should he attempt it?

And just then an extraordinary figure stepped out from behind a tree. It was a Jeeves-like figure, an African man carrying a silver tray with a tea service on it; teapot in a cosy, milk jug, sugar bowl with beaded cover and a delicate china cup. Was this a hallucination, an English drawing room in the African bush. But no, the butler poured a cup of tea for Duffy and said Senhor Pottie would like to speak to him when he had finished his tea.

Next Duffy was being led through the bush to a clearing where a tarpaulin was stretched some twenty feet above the ground, between four trees. The space beneath was walled with canvas, making a huge tent. Inside this tent an extraordinary Crusoe-like figure sat in an easy chair, bearded and wearing an assortment of tattered garments. He sprang to his feet with great geniality when Duffy appeared and shook his hand, introducing himself as Pottie Potgieter. The place was a jumble of old furniture, including four-poster beds, paraffin refrigerators and primus stoves. A brood of ragged children ran noisily about the place, jumping on the furniture, and Pottie's wife appeared from a corner that appeared to be a kitchen.

Duffy should on no account attempt the incline until it had stopped raining, Pottie said. He could easily come to grief. He should rather stay the night and set off again when conditions dried out.

Pottie was an Afrikaner who had gone wild in the Mozambique bush. He was actually a prospector looking for coal on behalf of a mining company but life in the bush had such an appeal he had become part of it. He had rifles and a shotgun and he hunted every day for the pot. His wife was a teacher and she was teaching the children. It was an idyllic existence and he had no intention of leaving. But he did enjoy talking to newcomers.

This was the first of many stopovers for Duffy on his way to Cahora Bassa. The children would give up their four-poster bed, eager to sleep in the cab of the lorry instead. He and Pottie would talk late into the night over Mozambican beer or the occasional bottle of whisky Duffy brought through. Pottie was delightful, irrepressible. He and his family had slotted in with the local community. Yes, Frelimo were present in the district but the locals had told them Pottie and his family were no harm at all and were not involved with the Portuguese authorities; no harm would come to them.

But the roadside oasis was to come to an end. The Portuguese authorities ordered Pottie to hand in his firearms because they were an incentive for Frelimo to raid. Pottie argued that he needed them to hunt for the pot, virtually every day. He had no fear of Frelimo, he said. But the authorities were insistent and eventually Pottie had to reluctantly end the idyll, sadly packing the family's belongings and setting off to wherever they came from in the Transvaal. Duffy never saw or heard of Pottie again but missed him sorely for the rest of his trucking stint.

Arrived at Salisbury one afternoon, Duffy recalled a girl he had met in Durban, and had a brief fling with, years before. She was a Rhodesian from Matopo, about forty miles outside Salisbury on the route to the border post at Nyamapanda. He found the Dunbar name in the telephone directory and made a call. Who should pick up the telephone but Georgia, the girl in question. He explained that he was passing through Salisbury and would like to see her.

She was delighted. He must spend the night at the ranch. She would drive in and fetch him.

No, he had transport, he said. He had a Mercedes. So she gave him directions.

"Is that the hay lorry, dear?" asked Georgia's mother as Duffy scrunched the Mercedes rig to a stop on the carefully raked driveway of the Dunbar ranch.

"No, it's just Peter. He said he was driving a Mercedes but …"

The mother, who was of German extraction, thought it a huge joke. It was the start of a resumed relationship that was to last years. Georgia had a flat in Salisbury, where she worked, and Duffy stayed there whenever he stopped over on his way to Mozambique or Zambia. Salisbury in those days had a vibrant night life and Duffy was in his element; a trucker one day, the next part of a sophisticated social circle. He slipped easily from his rig gear into the tuxedo he now had hanging in Georgia' flat.

Oddly enough, Georgia also featured (though in the most positive way) in the one serious mishap of Duffy's trucking career. He was on the way back from the Copperbelt. He had passed through the border post at Chirundu and was heading along the escarpment into Rhodesia when the front tyre of the Diamond-T blew. At first he thought it was an ambush – Zanu guerrilla activity had been on the increase in that district – but then a slewing of the giant vehicle told him otherwise. A steep drop of several hundred feet lay to his left. If he engaged the rear brakes – the normal approved method – the vehicle would straighten out then go into a spinning roll as it went over the side, that would carry on and on. If he applied the front brakes it would jack-knife and perhaps stop rolling. He hit the front brakes. The Diamond-T jack-knifed; they went over the edge; Duffy saw bush, sky, screen, then bush again. They stopped rolling. The tactic had worked. Duffy clambered from the cab, which was hanging at a drunken angle. He had a small cut on his ankle and he had lost one of his flip-flop sandals. Astonishingly, he was fine though the rig was in bad shape and there was a stench of spilled diesel fuel. He managed to open the bonnet and disconnected the batteries to avert the danger of a spark setting the rig on fire.

Then he climbed laboriously back to the road. From there the rig could not even be seen. What now? This was before the days of mobile phones. Traffic on this stretch of road was sparse because of the threat of Zanu ambushes. Would anybody stop for a lone figure at the roadside? He could be a decoy for an ambush. Then a vehicle came into view. It was a police Land Rover. Duffy waved it down enthusiastically.

Duffy had a great respect for the British South Africa Police. They combined the qualities of British justice and decency with the rough and ready values of the frontier. Often they had stopped his lorry and searched it, always with great courtesy and humour. They were performing a necessary task in an insurgency. Duffy always had with him a coolbox of drinks – never alcohol while on the road – and he always offered them to the police when they stopped him.

"Hello, it's the cold drink man," said the officer as he pulled up. "What are you doing out here on your own?"

Duffy explained. They took him to a police post, from which he telephoned head office in South Africa. A team would have to be sent to retrieve the rig and its cargo of copper cabling, take it all back on a lowbed lorry. Legally, it could not be left in Rhodesia. Then he phoned Georgia to tell her what had happened.

"No problem, I'll come and fetch you."

Then she was into her small Fiat and heading for the bush, after making a booking at a lodge near Mana Pools, which was close to where Duffy had crashed, one of the most scenic and sought-after spots in Rhodesia. The police were astonished as the grimy, dishevelled truck driver was picked up and whisked away by a cool and glamorous, highly sophisticated girl in a smart car.

"I'm afraid you've missed the game drive," said the receptionist as they booked in. "But if I were you I'd take a shower now, before they get back. We're having water problems and when they all switch on their showers at the same time it tends to just dry up."

It was much later. Duffy and Georgia were under the shower together. They were soaping each other. They heard the return of the game drive party. Then the water stopped spurting from the showerhead as the game drive people all simultaneously rushed for the showers. Duffy and Georgia were still covered in soapsuds. The tribulations of life in Africa.

****

Heavy-duty long-distance trucking had been an experience but it could never have been a long-term thing. Duffy returned to Durban. The word on the grapevine was that matters were deteriorating fast in Angola in the wake of the coup d'etat in Lisbon that removed from power the fascists who had ruled for so many decades. The new government was bent on decolonisation, and the process seemed headed for chaos. There was much at stake in the region – not just the oil, diamonds and coffee of Angola but also the copper of Zambia and Zaire (the new name given to the Congo). Colonel Mike Hoare was said to be negotiating a contract to police and protect the Benguela Railway, which ran right across Angola carrying the copper production of Zambia and Zaire to the southern ports of Benguela and Lobito for shipment overseas. Five Commando was said to be regrouping.

Meanwhile, a man had to make a living. Duffy went back into his previous role as a social photographer about Durban's nightspots. He increasingly began freelance newspaper photography as well, working mainly for the Sunday Tribune. He became a familiar figure on the touchline at rugby matches at King's Park, at major horseraces, at disaster scenes, at any kind of news event.

The Angola venture came to nothing. Newspaper photography became Duffy's main activity and he was eventually persuaded to join the permanent staff of the Sunday Tribune and its sister newspapers, the Daily News and the Natal Mercury. There he had remained – apart from an eventful interlude – until retirement.

14

PRESS PHOTOGRAPHER

Duffy became a kind of bull terrier of press photography. His combative character showed through. Not for him the sedate, acquiescent shot. If he had to shin up a drainpipe or climb a tree for it, so much the better. If the subject was unwilling and he had to snatch the shot, it was a bonus. And if he turned out to be violently antagonistic, everything moved onto a higher plane. Duffy never did mind a little aggro. Yet all of it was done with irrepressible good humour. And, very importantly, superb camera craft. He won many photographic awards, in all kinds of categories.

Duffy ensconced himself in a rambling Victorian double-storey, that became known as the Spook House, set in spacious grounds that had once been a small farm on the Berea, the high, wooded hill that looks out over Durban and the Indian Ocean. He had a cushy billet as caretaker on behalf of the old Durban family who owned the place. Georgia had joined him from Rhodesia. The gracious old place became a social gathering point. Old comrades from 5 Commando would drop in from time to time. Duffy kept a flock of raucous geese in the grounds, the best burglar alarm ever. When the neighbours complained about the noise, a young police constable arrived one morning to investigate.

"But these are my watchdogs," said Duffy.

"Dogs? The complaint said geese. Ag man, some of these people don't know what day of the week it is. Sorry to trouble you, hey." At which he drove off and Duffy heard nothing further. The idyll continued undisturbed.

Duffy was a busy man. He was working virtually full-time for the newspapers. He was roaming the restaurants and night clubs every evening, taking social pictures. He became a very well-known figure. If you frequented the night spots or watched rugby at King's Park or cricket at Kingsmead – and many did all three – you could not escape him. Every hotel or restaurant manager in the city knew him, every chef. The police would telephone him at all hours with tip-offs. Duffy had things pretty well sewn up.

This was the routine. He was also to experience regular spikes in his professional activity. It was afternoon when the Tribune newsdesk first heard of a case in the Supreme Court, fifty-six miles away in Pietermaritzburg. A roughneck coal miner from Newcastle, in Northern Natal, was being sued for divorce by his wife. The couple had two young boys, who he was badly maltreating. He would force them to box barefisted in the back garden until one of them had a bloody nose. He would then seize the so far unharmed one, hold him and force the other to hit him until he too had a bloody nose. Sometimes he thrashed both of them with a length of electric cable.

This charming fellow had lost a foot in a mining accident in Rhodesia and had a wooden stump instead of a foot, Long John Silver-style. But he made light of this disability. Now in Newcastle, he was a renowned bar-room brawler and he used his peg-leg to great advantage, kicking at his opponents with it, usually aiming for the crotch. It had become not a disability but a fearsome weapon.

The court had granted the wife a restraining order against his visiting the family home in Newcastle, which had led in turn to a charge against him of attempted murder. He had burst into the house causing a commotion, at which she telephoned the police. When they arrived, Peg-Leg had flung the dining room table at them through a glass window, then held a bread knife at the throat of one of the boys, threatening to kill him if the police did not leave. But they managed to overpower him, the boy was physically unharmed and the charge was laid.

In the matter before the court that day, the wife had taken pictures with a hidden camera of the bloodied boys after one of the back garden boxing matches instigated by Peg-Leg, before they washed off at a stone basin outside the back door. She had also photographed the electric flex used in the thrashings. These were handed in to the court as evidence and were part of the record. Duffy would be allowed to photograph them.

He and reporter Terry McElligott were told to get to Pietermaritzburg double-quick. To get the court record, photograph the pictures, photograph and interview the wife, get a photograph of Peg-Leg – and interview him if possible – and get back to Durban as soon as possible. Adding to the urgency was the fact that the Christmas long weekend was just a day off. The newspaper was in fact holding its wetstone – the Christmas party in the newspaper industry – the very next evening. The Tribune wanted that story and those pictures very urgently. Duffy and McElligott would be lucky if they got back in time for the wetstone. But such is life on a newspaper.

When they got to Pietermaritzburg, driven by a pool driver known to everyone simply as "Buthelezi" – he seemed not to use a Christian name – the court had adjourned hours earlier. The wife had left for Newcastle. Peg-Leg had not been there. But the clerk of the court gave them access to the court record, including the photographs, which Duffy copied.

Next stop Newcastle, several hours away by road. By the time they got there it was dark and raining. They found the wife's house in the town and were about to go in when they noticed a four-wheel drive vehicle parked outside. Just then the front door flung open and a man with a wooden leg came storming out. It was their first encounter with Peg-Leg, there in defiance of the court's restraining order. He ignored Duffy and McElligott, jumped into the vehicle and sped away with a screech of tyres.

They went in, introduced themselves and settled down to interview and photograph the wife, who was wholly co-operative though in a badly shaken state. Also present was a squat, lugubrious fellow who had little to say for himself. He turned out to be the wife's brother. He looked so much like Oddjob the character in the James Bond film, *Goldfinger*, that Duffy and McElligott named him so right away.

They still needed a photograph of Peg-Leg. Where was he to be found? He was on a relative's farm outside Newcastle, the wife said, about 11 miles away. She gave them directions. They drove off into the dark and the rain, Buthelezi at the wheel, then spent an hour or more driving around the farm roads, totally lost. The wife's directions had meant nothing. Better to check into the hotel, get something to eat then try again early next day.

It had been a long and tiring day. Duffy needed a beer or two (McElligott was teetotal). It was almost ten o'clock, which was when the bar closed at the Holiday Inn – so early because the miners otherwise became troublesome and were likely to be late for their shift next day. Duffy managed to order himself four pints and carry them to the lounge. In the lobby they encountered a familiar figure. It was Oddjob. He had come for a beer but was just too late. He seemed at first not to remember who they were.

"Do you want a beer?"

"Ja, I want a beer."

"Join us then, I've got a few."

Over a couple of beers, Oddjob remembered who they were. Yes, he knew the farm where Peg-Leg was staying. Yes, of course he could take them there. After finishing the beers they were on the farm roads again, the rain pelting down. But Oddjob took them directly to the farm without any trouble. The farmhouse was L-shaped and surrounded by a picket fence. Duffy had a shrewd idea that this was going to be one of those tricky flash-and-run jobs.

"Keep the car engine running," he told Buthelezi. "Don't switch off."

In those days they used the old-fashioned Metz flash that was attached to the battery by a length of flex. Duffy had the camera in his right hand, the flex running down through the sleeve of his safari suit to the battery in his pocket. He reckoned that if it came to a physical confrontation with Peg-Leg it would be fairly even – a one-legged man against another with only one arm free.

The vehicle stopped and four or five massive dogs starting bounding about, barking. But Duffy has a way with animals and managed to quiet them. Also, they seemed to recognise Oddjob. The three of them made for the front door in the pouring rain. Oddjob knocked.

"Wie's daar?" a voice called from inside. (Who's there?)

"Dis die menere van die pers." (It's the gentlemen from the press).

At which lights seemed to switch on everywhere. Standing in a large plateglass window, staring out, was the magnificent sight of Peg-Leg in nothing but his boxer shorts, the wooden stump clearly visible. It would make a wonderful shot. Then Peg-Leg was gone, stumping around the corner inside and making for the front door. Duffy waited. There he was. Flash!

"Let's go!"

They got to the car, Peg-Leg stumping behind them. But Buthelezi had switched off the engine and was taking a nap, the driver's seat reclining well back. It had been a long day.

Peg-Leg was right behind them. Duffy suddenly remembered he had a 500mm mirror lens on the back seat of the car. It must not come to any harm. Peg-Leg must not be allowed into the car. He locked the front passenger's door, then the rear door, Peg-Leg practically breathing down his neck. Then he darted round behind and locked the other rear door.

"Start the vehicle, Buthelezi!"

Peg-Leg was virtually chasing Duffy round the car. But when he got to the unlocked driver's door, he reached in and half-pulled Buthelezi out. Then he slammed the car door three or four times against his head. Then he reached in, took the keys out of the ignition and flung them out into the night.

The fat was now well and truly in the fire. No escape. Buthelezi ran off dazed into the dark. Duffy turned to face his assailant. At least he knew which was his wooden leg. He swept his good leg away with a karate kick. Peg-Leg went down like a ninepin. Duffy was onto him, throttling him with his one free hand. A commotion of male voices came from the farmhouse.

"Bring my rewolwer!" shouted Peg-Leg.

The situation was going from bad to worse. Duffy sprang up and grabbed McElligott by the arm.

"Let's go!"

They ran off into the dark, straight into a barbed wire fence. Then they climbed through that into a ploughed field and started staggering through the morass. Then it turned out the dogs were with them – with them, not pursuing them. Trained to hunt, they seemed to think it was another hunting expedition, a bit of night-time poaching.

"Keep going! We've got to keep going. We must stay off the road and footpaths."

Sure enough, vehicles were starting up at the farmhouse. Hunting spotlights played about. Hunting rifles cracked in the darkness, aimed at nothing. The roads were not a good place to be.

"Where are we running to?"

"See that light over there?" Sure enough, a solitary light was discernible between the squalls of rain, in the middle distance. "We'll see what's there."

McElligott said something inaudible.

"What's that?"

"I said the office will never believe this," he panted.

Then a new sound joined that of the farm vehicles, the deep-throated roar of a different engine. It sounded as if a tank or something had joined the pursuit.

The light was closer now. It seemed to be from some sort of government pump station. Living quarters seemed to be attached. They knocked at the door, which was answered by an absolutely startled technician. They explained that they needed to contact the police to lay a charge of assault. Could they use his telephone?

"Ja, we've been looking for you okes," said the desk sergeant in Newcastle. The people on the farm phoned. They're laying a charge against you. Where are you?"

"Look, it's the other way round. We're laying a charge of assault against them."

"Okay, okay. Where are you?"

The mystery tank was soon explained as a police car drew up at the pumping station. Driving about on the farm roads, it had lost its exhaust system on a cattlegrid. Inside the medium-sized vehicle were four enormously fat Afrikaner policemen. To fit in, Duffy and McElligott, each had to sit on the lap of a policeman as they drove back to Newcastle, the roar of the exhaust making conversation impossible. There was something surreal about it, a fitting finale to events on the farm.

In the police station, the officers repeated that Duffy and McElligott were to be charged. They counter-argued that they were the ones who were going to press charges. They would have to wait for the station commander to arrive, the constables said. This officer never did make an appearance. They sat all night in the charge office, dozing on chairs.

Came the dawn and Buthelezi appeared. As he ran off in the dark he had taken off his white shirt so he would not be visible. He now had it on again and it was caked with blood; his face was a mass of contusions where Peg-Leg had smashed the car door against it. But he had done the sensible thing by making for the police station to report the incident. The police on duty began to waver. It looked as if the newspaper team might have a case after all. But still there was no station commander.

Duffy put through a call to the newsdesk in Durban to report what had happened. He was startled by the reply: "Well at least we know where you are and you're safe."

Safe? While the rest of the staff would be whooping it up at the wetstone, Duffy, McElligott and Buthelezi could be starting to spend the weekend in police cells. They were somewhat irked.

However, the sight of Buthelezi's injuries seemed to have mollified the police somewhat. They agreed to drive the three back to the farm to retrieve their vehicle. But Duffy insisted that a breakdown vehicle should follow. It would almost certainly be needed because the ignition keys had been hurled away into the night.

A strange little procession set out. The police car, its exhaust still blowing mightily (though with only two fat constables in it this time), followed by a breakdown tow truck When they got there, the tow truck was indeed needed. Not only had Peg-Leg let down all four tyres, he had opened the bonnet and smashed the distributor. The vehicle was immobile.

This seemed to particularly irritate the policemen, whose attitude to the case now switched entirely. They went into the farmhouse, roused Peg-Leg from his slumbers and ordered him to pump each tyre himself. It was exquisite revenge for Duffy to watch Peg-Leg as he balanced on his stump and worked the footpump with his good leg, glowering at Duffy's impersonation of a Cheshire Cat.

The vehicle was towed back to Newcastle and taken to a repair shop. Then they waited again at the police station for the absent station commander. Buthelezi went out to snooze more comfortably in the car. The police said not a thing.

Duffy said quietly: "Let's just go."

"We can't do that!"

"These guys are sick of the whole thing. We haven't been charged. Let's go."

They walked out quietly and got into the car. Buthelezi started it and they drove sedately out of the police yard. No blue lights or sirens pursued them. They never heard another word about charges for trespassing or anything else. But they did have all the material they had set out to get. It made a sensational picture spread in the Tribune that Sunday. Duffy still rates it one of his more memorable assignments.

***

Another case of the unwilling photographic subject turned out rather differently. In the Eastern Cape port city of East London, an ogre of a man with a reputation for violent racism was on trial on 22 counts of murder. A member of the extreme right-wing Afrikaner Weerstandsbeweging (Afrikaner Resistance Movement), he was also a security guard. He was accused of responding to silent alarms when they went off at factories, then deliberately gunning down the culprits – invariably black youths – without making any attempt to arrest them. At one factory three youths had broken in but he spotted only two, who he gunned down. The third hid and survived to tell the tale. The mills of justice ground slow but exceeding fine, even in apartheid South Africa, and this man was eventually prosecuted.

Huge – well over six feet – and bulky, he had a flowing black beard and burning, coal-black eyes. He epitomised the right-wing zealot of the day and was highly aggressive. He had already taken a swing at the Daily News East London correspondent when he tried to photograph him at a previous court appearance and it was felt that back-up was now needed. Duffy was detailed to take the early morning "milk run" flight from Durban, that stopped off at East London, Port Elizabeth and Cape Town, returning that evening. Because the booking was late and economy class was full, they had to send Duffy business class.

Duffy is not a habitual early riser but was at the airport at crack of dawn. Discovering that he was entitled to the luxury of the business class lounge, he discovered there also that everything was free, included in the price of the ticket. He had some time to wait and decided an Irish coffee would go down well and properly open his eyes. It went down very well. It was for free. He ordered another. Then there was time for just another before his flight was called. He boarded, spoke for a while to the passenger beside him as they were in flight, then dozed off. He awoke as they were landing. He had no hold luggage so was able to stroll straight to the car hire desk and collect the keys for the vehicle that had been booked for him. But there was no booking. This was most strange. Duffy retrieved the booking voucher from his camera bag and handed it to the girl behind the desk.

"This is for East London."

"Yes, that's right."

"You're in Port Elizabeth."

Duffy was not familiar with the airports of the Eastern Cape. It was those Irish coffees. He had slept right through the landing and take-off at East London. The Daily News East London correspondent would be waiting for him. He had a court case to attend. He telephoned Durban to explain what had happened. He got through to assistant editor Peter Davis and explained.

"Well, I hope you've got a tele-lens," Davis guffawed.

"I've got to get there by road. There's no flight until this evening."

"Use your initiative. I know you."

Just then the car hire girl came bustling up. One of her colleagues had to drive a car to Port Elizabeth. She could give Duffy a lift. Problem solved. They set off, Duffy distracted by the shapely pair of legs under a short skirt that she hitched even shorter to make pedal control easier. Duffy is a good listener to women. By the time they reached the Fish River Sun, where she planned to have breakfast, he already knew all about her problems with her current boyfriend and was offering sympathetic advice.

At the Fish River Sun, who should he encounter but the manager, an old friend who had until recently managed one of the group's Durban hotels. He pressed on Duffy a coupon for use in the casino and Duffy – by no means an instinctive gambler – wandered through and began playing the slot machines. By the time he joined the car hire girl at the breakfast table he had amassed R400 in winnings, which he handed to her in gratitude for the lift and insisted that if she didn't take it she give it to her boyfriend, so long as he bought her flowers. The trip was picking up in jollity – but the racist ogre still lay ahead.

Arrived in East London, the car hire girl dropped Duffy at the courthouse. There he met up with the Daily News correspondent who told him the court would adjourn shortly. The ogre would walk down a certain corridor with his attorney to get to the car park. They worked out a plan. This would have to be a flash and run operation. Duffy would jump out from around a corner, take one shot – zap! – then make his escape while they were still blinking in astonishment.

Footsteps approached. Duffy sprang round the corner camera poised. Approaching him were a bearded giant and an attorney who he vaguely recognised from somewhere.

"Yislaaik, Duffy! What are you doing here?" The attorney turned to his client. "This is one of your guys. He invaded the Seychelles and hijacked the Air India plane." (This was soon after an incident to be recounted in later chapters).

The racist ogre shook Duffy enthusiastically by the hand. Beaming, he posed for a range of photographs: smiling, snarling, looking contemplative. From a distance the Daily News East London correspondent and the rest of the press corps looked on in astonishment.

That evening Duffy boarded the evening flight back to Durban. By chance he found himself seated beside the same man who had flown down with him from Durban.

"What a coincidence. But didn't you fly on to Port Elizabeth? How was your day?"

Duffy thought about it. Landing in the wrong city. Breakfasting with a charming girl. Winning at the casino. Then a coup in getting pictures of the racist ogre. "Oh not too bad, up and down. Pretty good on the whole."

***

Duffy was leopard crawling along the hospital corridor with his camera and lenses. He had to get past the desk where the matron sat as a sentinel. He had just about made it when a nurse came down the corridor pushing a trolley. She shrieked. The game was up. The matron was there, hissing with indignation. Duffy was summarily marched out of the hospital by the porters and told not to show his face again.

It was a tragic and extraordinary case. A light aircraft from Johannesburg was lost in bad weather in the Drakensberg foothills.

On board with the pilot were a woman, who had a relationship with him, and her young son who was asleep in the back of the aircraft. Eventually the aircraft ran out of fuel and they crashed into woodland in a remote spot. Because there was no fuel, there was no fire. The pilot was killed instantly, the woman not. She lived for two days, cradled by the boy who had escaped unhurt. Eventually the wreck was found by a forest ranger and the boy was rushed to hospital in Ladysmith suffering dehydration and various forms of trauma.

It made headlines everywhere. The hospital issued regular bulletins on the boy's condition. But press access to him was (understandably) refused. But this was the kind of challenge Duffy simply could not resist. Hence the leopard crawling toward the boy's ward. He wanted a picture of him lying in bed. A good story demanded a good picture.

Nothing daunted by his expulsion, Duffy crept around the outside of the single-storey hospital, accompanied by a reporter, and found what he thought would be the right ward. A large-paned horizontal swivel window was half-open. He clambered up and squeezed through the open space. Sure enough, he had the right ward. There was the perfect shot; the boy in bed, the nurses attending to him. Quietly he took the shot – no flash – and slid backwards.

Then – Bang! Crash! – and a tinkling of glass. The window had swung down on his head. The place was instantly in uproar, boots pounded. Duffy – blood streaming from various minor lacerations – quickly removed the film, slipped it to the reporter and put in a new one. Then the police were there, led by a major.

"I'm going to lock you up!"

"For what? The window was an accident."

"Give me your film!"

Duffy wound off the film, opened the camera and handed him the spool. Then the major marched he and the reporter to the gates of the hospital.

"Now you just get out of here, you hear? I don't want to see you again." As they turned to leave, he held up the spool and pulled down a lower eyelid. "You think I don't know this is the wrong spool?"

Duffy had got away with it again. His instinctive empathy for animals has been noted. Often it also extends to policemen.

***

Duffy's gallantry toward ladies has also been noted. There was a noted incident when he and a reporter dropped off at the newspaper group's Pietermaritzburg bureau while on their way to an assignment in Northern Natal. They needed to use the telephone.

Inside the editorial office sat a gorgeous brunette, well-stacked, hair coiffed and manicured in every detail. She tapped daintily at a typewriter with long, painted fingernails. On her desk was a red carnation in a glass of water.

"Who gave you the flower?"

She ignored Duffy.

"I said who gave you the flower?"

"Mind your own business!"

"He's a cheapskate."

"What? How dare you!

"One carnation? He's a cheapskate."

"He's a man who loves me very much. He sends me a carnation every day!"

"He's still a cheapskate. A girl like you is worth a dozen red roses."

At which she stomped off to complain to the bureau chief, Johnny Odendaal.

"Go easy, chaps, she's a bit highly strung. I told her you're going soon. You are going aren't you?"

Driving out of Pietermaritzburg, Duffy and his companion discussed the lack of humour and tolerance so often to be found in otherwise highly attractive women. They stopped at a red traffic light. They were outside a florist's shop. An idea dawned.

They went in and ordered a huge bouquet of consummate vulgarity. Everything went into it: roses, carnations, lilies, snapdragons, lavender, banana fronds, ivy. They explained to the counter assistant that they would pay cash but they wanted the bouquet to be delivered, with a COD slip – cash on delivery – to a certain lady at the Daily News Pietermaritzburg bureau in Longmarket Street.

The girl reporter once again went rushing to the long-suffering Johnny Odendaal. He telephoned the florist's and the situation was explained. Meanwhile, Duffy and his companion headed with a lightness of spirit for Northern Natal. "Hau!" said driver Moses. "You gentlemen are mad!"

***

Duffy was a familiar, chunky figure as he ran up and down the touchline at Currie Cup rugby matches at King's Park. On one occasion he actually joined the game.

It was Natal versus Northern Transvaal. A wind was swirling in the stadium. Natal put up a high kick toward the touchline. Northerns flyhalf Naas Botha got under it, the ball swirling with the wind. Duffy was on the spot, focused on the ball for the moment Botha would take it and a Natal chaser would slam into him. So enthusiastically did Duffy follow the ball that he did not realise the swirl had taken it slightly infield again.

Next thing he crashed into Naas Botha who went flying, the ball free for Natal to grab and wreak havoc. It happened right in front of the main grandstand. The crowd cheered. They cheered again as Duffy turned and gave a sweeping bow.

Botha complained bitterly afterwards that Natal won with 16 men on the field. He even mentioned the incident in a later book. But the following weekend the Sunday Tribune published a photograph of Duffy on the field at King's Park, snarling in a scrumcap, a ball under one arm and handing off with a camera in the other hand. He was becoming a highly recognisable figure.

***

Duffy's duties regularly took him to the horseraces, notably the Durban July Handicap. He had perfected a technique to shoot the photofinish with his own camera, standing at the winning post and getting the instant the winner got its nose across the line ahead of the others. But nothing could compare with the drama and excitement of an occasion when Duffy himself flashed past the winning post.

The occasion was caused by an incident some years earlier when three characters who might have stepped from the pages of Damon Runyon conspired to shoot the July Handicap favourite. They were bookmaker Sonny Chizzlet, a small-time hoodlum named Monty Labuschagne and a night club bouncer named Johnny Nel.

It was Nel who eventually fired a shot from a .22-calibre weapon into the rump of the odds-on favourite, Sea Cottage, from above as he passed under a culvert on his way to exercise on the beach. It caused near-hysteria throughout Natal. But Sea Cottage seemed to simply absorb the attack; the bullet was never extracted, the wound healed and he did not scratch from the July. He went on to run a place amid high emotion from the punters.

A sensational trial followed and security from then on became a very big issue in the run-up to the Durban July. The horses were no longer kept in the Greyville stables but at Summerveld, an equestrian centre at Shongweni, some distance from Durban.

That year's race was a few weeks off when the Sunday Tribune received information from a credible source that a shot had been fired (unsuccessfully) at the favourite up at Summerveld. He and other heavily backed horses had been moved to Greyville for security reasons. It was a Saturday afternoon, nobody was available to confirm or deny the story – the racing fraternity were all at another meeting at Clairwood – so it seemed the best thing was to investigate on the spot.

Duffy and a reporter entered the virtually empty Greyville racecourse and walked down the track past the main grandstand. Then they spotted some activity. Three racehorses were being exercised in a small ring. They approached; Duffy had his camera ready.

Then suddenly each was grabbed by the wrist in an iron grip. A Zulu security guard had got them from behind. He was one of those short, stocky Zulus – built like a brick shithouse, to use the Australian idiom – with arms like another man's legs. There was no escaping that grip. But he needed to get the handcuffs on his belt, so he let go of Duffy – at which Duffy performed a western roll over the railing behind him and set off in the direction he had come from, cameras and lenses whirling about him on their leather straps like mini-satellites in orbit. The guard let go of the reporter, drew his truncheon and set off after him.

There they were, haring down the main straight and past the photofinish camera, the stands empty and silent in spite of the drama being enacted – a photographer with cameras and lenses whirling about him in orbit, a Zulu security guard with truncheon raised, both of them sprinting. It was better than the Keystone Kops. The track veered right. Duffy jumped over the rail and carried on straight, headed for the racecourse gates. The security guard followed.

At the Durban Bowling Club, just across the road from the Greyville Racecourse entrance, they were holding the South African Bowls Championships. It was pretty decorous stuff: immaculate greens, white flannels, the clicking of the woods; a hum of appreciation. Then proceedings were interrupted by Duffy sprinting across the main green, pursued by a Zulu security guard in hobnailed boots, baton raised. Duffy ran into the clubhouse, slammed the door closed then put his shoulder to it from inside. The security guard hammered at it with his baton

"What the hell is this?" somebody in the press box asked.

"I've no idea," Alan Kitson, sports editor of Duffy's sister newspaper, the Daily News, replied quite truthfully.

The security guard suddenly ran out of steam. The job was done, he seemed to tell himself, and he turned away to make his way back to the racecourse, thoroughly blown. On the way he encountered the reporter and gave him a cheery wave. The fun was over. But Greyville had never seen a finish like it.

* * *

It is possible at times to look askance at some of Duffy's activities; the intrusiveness that sometimes accompanied his insistence of getting the picture, come hell or high water. In counter-balance, most times those who objected deserved to be intruded upon, it served the public interest. And there were times when his tenacity served the interest of third parties.

One afternoon he was sent with a reporter to a horrific lift accident that had happened just a block or so away from the old Newspaper House in Field Street. It was indeed a horror scene. A man had got into a lift on the third floor, pressed the "down" button then had second thoughts and opened the door again to step out. This should have stopped the lift. But it did not. The lift kept on going down and he was cut in two.

It was a scene of unbelievable grisliness. The lift had eventually stopped and on the third floor the mangled upper half of the man's body was to be found entangled with the lift's headgear. One floor down, a hysterical woman was sharing the lift with the victim's legs and lower trunk.

The police on the scene – themselves shocked – refused pointblank to allow Duffy to take photographs. He took the stairs down a floor and nobody stopped him photographing the victim's legs being taken away in a body bag.

Back upstairs he went. Another police officer seemed to be in charge. Duffy approached him: "Look, I can give you photographs for the inquest." The policeman considered. "Okay, go ahead."

Duffy got his gruesome shots (none of which were used by the newspaper, apart from the body bag shot from the floor below). But they did prove crucial for the inquest to determine that the lift had malfunctioned. The building's insurance company paid the victim's family a million rands (a truly massive sum at that time) the very same day.

***

Such was Duffy's lifestyle and modus operandi: gracious living on the Berea and a full social life; a trawling of the nightspots for social photographs; and hard news photo-journalism wherever it presented itself, undertaken with zest and an insistence that work had to be fun. It could seemingly continue indefinitely, except that events in the Indian Ocean were to deflect him on another course.

SEYCHELLES INVASION

The Seychelles group is an archipelago of 155 luxuriant tropical islands in the Indian Ocean, north-east of Madagascar and about 990 miles east of Kenya. The three main islands are Mahe, Praslin and La Digue; the rest are mainly small and uninhabited. The climate is humid though healthy and the vegetation includes the unique cocos du mer, a palm whose fruit bears a most suggestive resemblance to the curvaceous nether regions of a woman. The islands' luxuriance and lack of disturbance from natural forces and pestilences has led many to speculate that they are the original Garden of Eden.

The islands were a sporadic transit point between Africa and Asia in the early days, and there are indications that Maldivian and Arab traders might well have settled there a very long time ago. The islands were discovered by the Portuguese in the 17th century, on their way to India, and they appear also to have occasionally been used as a pirate base until the 18th century when they were colonised by France. Planters produced cotton, coconut oil, spices coffee and sugarcane, as well as food crops to support the local population, which consisted of the planters themselves and slaves they had imported to work the fields. It was this human settlement that produced the French/Creole population that inhabits the Seychelles today.

Britain took control of the islands during the Napoleonic wars, and this was formalised in the post-Napoleonic settlement. The Seychelles became a crown colony in 1903 and sixty-odd years of soporific existence were to follow, with representative government dominated by planter politics, the islands very much on the margins of world attention, barely touched even by two world wars.

This was to change as Britain began in the 1960s to divest herself of her African possessions; as the tremors of decolonisation reached out even across the ocean to these remote islands; and as the Indian Ocean began, very gradually, to become a theatre of the Cold War. Political parties formed in the Seychelles: notably the Seychelles Democratic Party, led by James Mancham, a successful businessman with close connections to London, Paris and other western capitals, who favoured the closest association with Britain; and the Socialist Seychelles People's United Party, led by Albert Rene, a lawyer who had been educated in Britain and who had become involved in Labour Party politics there. He campaigned for complete independence from Britain. Mancham won elections in 1964, becoming chief minister of the colony, and again in 1970 and 1974, gaining a small majority in votes but a large one in terms of seats in the legislature because of the "first past the post" electoral system.

By 1975 Mancham switched position, realising Britain was lukewarm to ideas of a continuing close constitutional link with the Seychelles, which would have been absolutely counter to developments in continental Africa. He joined Rene in calling for full independence and the Democratic Party and the Socialist People's United Party went into a coalition. Mancham became Prime Minister. With independence as a republic within the Commonwealth in 1976, Mancham became President and Rene Prime Minister.

Less than a year later, Mancham was in London for a Commonwealth Conference when sixty supporters of the Socialist People's United Party, who had trained militarily in Tanzania, staged a bloodless coup d'etat on Mahe, the main island, seizing all the key points and installing Rene as President. While it is not entirely clear whether Rene was involved in plotting the coup from the start, he subsequently co-operated with enthusiasm, allowing himself to be installed as President, bringing in a large Tanzanian military force, introducing a new constitution proclaiming a one-party socialist state, setting up press censorship and abolishing fee-paying religious schools. A Seychellois army was created for the first time ever and a large security apparatus was established. North Korean military advisers appeared on the scene. Political education was introduced. For the easy-going Seychellois this was a severe disruption of their hitherto humble but carefree lifestyle.

The Seychelles islands were by no means strategically vital to either side in the Cold War. But the Indian Ocean was increasingly becoming a theatre of that struggle for hearts and minds – and resources – and any incremental change was a propaganda victory for one side and a setback for the other. There was the possibility that Soviet influence in the Seychelles could start to counter the strategic effect of the United States military base that had been built on the British-owned island of Diego Garcia. Rene's seizing of power and setting up of an authoritarian one-party socialist regime seemed a classic example of the Kremlin's then-current Brezhnev doctrine: seizing any advantage in the Third World so long as the costs were not too high. It was a setback to the ideals and founding principles of the Commonwealth. South Africa, increasingly isolated in the world as international pressures built up against the policy of apartheid, had fears of losing its national airline's landing rights in the Seychelles. And James Mancham and his supporters in exile had every interest in reversing what had been most certainly an illegal and unconstitutional seizing of power. All kinds of groupings had reason to wish for Rene's removal from power.

A Seychelles Liberation Committee had been established in Paris. A *Mouvement pour la Resistance* had been announced, supposedly having the support of Seychelles islanders themselves. The Seychelles Liberation Committee was said to have held discussions with the South African government. It was a classically grey climate of spooks and skulduggery, all kinds of clandestine comings and goings. The new Seychelles government was understandably nervous.

Five Commando had meanwhile been secretly regrouping in South Africa. It initially had nothing at all to do with the Seychelles. As noted elsewhere, Angola, on the West Coast of Africa, was approaching crisis as the departure date of the colonial Portuguese approached, no stable transitionary government having been put in place. Two copper-producing countries, Zambia and Zaire (as the Congo was then called), relied absolutely for the exporting of their copper on the Benguella Railway, which ran the whole way south-west across Angola to the ports of Lobito and Benguella. The Benguella line was not just an export artery vital to the economies of Zambia and Zaire – and significant enough for the Angolan economy also – it was a dividing line between the territory of the *Movement Popular dos Povos da Angola* (MPLA – who were eventually to seize power in Angola, backed by Cuban/Soviet forces) and Dr Jonas Savimbi's *Union Nationale do Indpendencia Total da Angola* (Unita – which was soon to launch a new guerrilla war that would last decades).

Trains of the steam-driven Benguella Railway had regularly come under fire from MPLA and Unita (mainly Unita) guerrillas as it traversed Angola during the years leading up to the military coup d'etat in Lisbon that led to the Portuguese withdrawal. A rail-mounted armoured car bristling with machineguns always ran along the track ahead. The train itself always carried a platoon or two of troops in case of ambush. Who would play this role when the Portuguese left?

Colonel Mike Hoare, founder and commander of Five Commando in the Congo, had been approached by various interests in Angola. He was trying to negotiate a deal in which a mercenary force under his command would take responsibility for securing the safety of the Benguella Railway when the Portuguese left, assuring the continued flow of copper production from Zambia and Zaire to the outside world. It would involve not just riding shotgun on the train, it would also involve patrols along the route to eliminate sabotage of the track. It would be a massive undertaking and Hoare would have to recruit not just his Five Commando veterans but as many Portuguese ex-servicemen as possible, to overcome the language barrier.

Duffy had never actually served under Hoare. But Hoare sought him out, he living at Hilton, just outside Pietermaritzburg, the Natal capital, and Duffy being less than sixty miles away in Durban. Tentative sounding-out and recruitment began, in Johannesburg and Durban. Duffy increasingly won Hoare's confidence. The Wild Geese were gathering again.

But the Angolan project evaporated as Angola exploded into a civil war that was to last the best part of three decades and the Benguella Railway was blasted out of existence. (Zambian and Zairean copper exports now had to follow a tortuous and hideously expensive rail route through Zimbabwe, down to the South African port of East London). But the tentative mustering was already in place when Hoare was approached by representatives of James Mancham for assistance in restoring him to power in the Seychelles.

Popular myth has it that the Seychelles invasion in 1981 was plotted by a group of boozy ex-mercenaries who used to gather regularly at the Riviera Hotel of an evening, a popular establishment on Durban's palm-lined Esplanade, looking out over the harbour. The truth is that almost all involved had already been approached with a view to the Benguella Railway project. It was just that the project changed. Colonel Hoare himself never went near the Riviera. The hotel did have as a barman a former Rhodesian special forces man, who had indeed been approached but had no idea what the mission actually would be. He and friends, some of whom had also been approached, became garrulous as the evenings wore on. But they knew nothing and were plotting nothing. It was not until Colonel Hoare called a meeting of all who had been approached, at the Coastlands holiday flats, also in Durban, that they were briefed as to the target and the objectives and were given the opportunity to drop out if they wished, which a few did.

Duffy initially was not enthusiastic about the Seychelles mission. It seemed almost harebrained; it was being put together on a shoestring budget which seemed to be constantly shrinking. But eventually he warmed to Hoare's enthusiasm. Also, he was approached by one Martin Dolinchek (whose name will crop up again), a senior officer in South Africa's National Intelligence Service (which was still known to most people by its unfortunate original acronym BOSS – Bureau Of State Security) to perform a mission on behalf of the government. When the coup happened, Duffy was to go to the Soviet embassy (from which the staff would presumably have fled) and photograph every document he could find. The mission now became potentially very lucrative indeed.

Ordinary members of the group were to be paid $10 000 (US) for the mission, which was expected to last about ten days. As second-in-command, Duffy would get $30 000. But, in terms of Dolinchek's offer, BOSS would pay him an extra $30 000. In 1981 values this was significant money, even for the lowest ranks.

About 50 individuals signed up. Only about half a dozen were former Five Commando men. The rest were mostly either former personnel of the Rhodesian special forces or serving members of the South African special forces, at the time on the reserve list but still liable for call-up. It would probably be an exaggeration to say the group were imbued with any particular enthusiasm for unseating an undemocratic regime that had come to power by force. Though Colonel Hoare almost certainly entertained such notions, and he did spell them out at the briefing, these tough recruits are more likely to have thought in terms of another mission against "the enemy" which beset South Africa on every side – plus the bonus they would get out of it. None had any doubt but that the mission had the blessing of the South African government.

BATTLE PLAN

The battle plan for the invasion of the Seychelles must surely be one of the most unusual since the Wooden Horse of Troy. It must be the first time in the annals of military history that an invading force has checked through immigration control and taken its weapons through customs and excise. But then "invasion" is probably the wrong word. This was not to be an invasion in the classic sense but an infiltration, after which the mercenary force would lie low, waiting for a signal from the Seychellois Resistance, at which it would seize the island's armoury, the radio station and various other key points and hold the situation while the Resistance took control and James Mancham and his government-in-exile flew in from Kenya. It was the alternative to a seaborne landing and assault, which would require greater numbers; the organisation of craft; great expense; likely casualties; and would be far more easily open to detection, leading to failure. Financial and other resources were meagre.

The plan was a follows:

- An advance party of eight (including one woman) should fly in posing as tourists and business people. They should thoroughly reconnoitre the main island, noting the disposition of troops,

Tanzanians in particular, and heavy weapons; the disposition of the armoury at the main barracks; and the disposition of the radio station and government buildings. The men should take with them through immigration and customs cut-down AK-47 automatic rifles and two magazines each of ammunition, concealed in false bottoms to their bags. (In the event, Martin Dolinchek, of BOSS, also flew in just ahead of the advance party, also posing as a tourist).

- The main party should meet at Jan Smuts airport, Johannesburg, posing as members of a charity called the Ancient and Honourable Order of Frothblowers International, on their way to the Seychelles to shower gifts on needy children and hospital patients and to have a jolly time doing it.

- They would noisily board a bus bearing the logo of the Ancient and Honourable Order of Frothblowers International and head for the Holiday Inn at Ermelo, in the Eastern Transvaal, making merry all the way.

- At Ermelo, each member of the force would take delivery of a specially designed luggage bag with a false bottom, in which would be concealed a cut-down AK-47 and two magazines of ammunition.

- Next day they would reboard the bus and head for Mbabane, in Swaziland (a landlocked former British protectorate), where they would go to the airport and board a normal Air Swaziland flight for the Seychelles, maintaining the atmosphere of noisy bonhomie.

- On arrival at Mahe airport, in the Seychelles, they would go through immigration and customs as normal tourists. Airport buses would take them to the different hotels on the island into which they would have been booked.

- They would surreptitiously make contact with the advance party, note their reconnaissance details and familiarise themselves with the disposition of the target to which they had been assigned for when the uprising began. All this to be done within a boisterous atmosphere of tourists having fun.
- When the signal came, make for the assigned target, the armoury at the Tanzanian barracks at one end of the airport runway being a key one. The strike should be at a time of changing guards, when one set of Tanzanian troops had handed in their weapons and the next set had not yet collected theirs. (Duffy, of course, also had to head for the Soviet embassy to take photographs on behalf of BOSS).
- Seize the radio station and play pre-recorded tapes by James Mancham in which he declares a successful counter-coup and appeals to the Seychellois people to stay calm and support his legitimate government.
- Secure the airport for the arrival of Mancham from Kenya.

It all sounded so simple. How could anything go wrong?

THE FROTHBLOWERS

The advance party had flown into the Seychelles, taking their weapons through customs and excise without incident. The main group gathered, under Duffy's command, at Jan Smuts airport on November 24, 1981, some having flown in from Durban, others having made their way from Johannesburg and surrounds. Several men in dark glasses – spooks from BOSS – watched proceedings from a distance. Duffy was nervous. His men had a distinctly military look about them, short back and sides haircuts, fit and tanned from the outdoors life. Once they boarded the bus he urged them to let their hair down, have a few drinks and enjoy themselves like lads out on the spree. Also, not to engage with outsiders once they got to the Holiday Inn at Ermelo; not get into conversation with anyone. Just look as if they were having a good time with the boys.

They reached Ermelo without incident then, as they went in through the front door into the reception lobby, Duffy heard himself being hailed: "Duffy, what the hell are you doing here?" His blood ran cold. It was an assistant manager from the Durban Holiday Inn, who he knew well. He had been transferred to Ermelo.

Duffy airily explained that he was on a charity jaunt with the Frothblowers, carefully giving away nothing about their destination. The hotelier pulled down a lower eyelid – he knew Duffy's past – but said nothing. The group had not yet all of them booked into the hotel when an incident occurred that could have scuppered the whole mission.

The men had been told not to engage with outsiders, but engagement suddenly occurred with a vengeance. A group of Frothblowers were still sitting in the hotel lobby waiting their turn to be checked in, when an attractive blonde caught their eye. She was sitting with a dumpy older man, who they guessed must be her sugar daddy. They started discussing the couple and laughing about the probable relationship; the man overheard the drift of their conversation and strode across indignantly. At which a highly decorated South African special forces man stood up and punched him several times in the face and tummy, giving him a bleeding nose and split lip and blood all over his clothes.

Duffy was horrified. He followed the couple up to their bedroom, and peeled off large denomination notes as he apologised for the conduct of his highly strung companion and asked them to please get clothing dry-cleaned at his expense; take his lady out to dinner at the best restaurant in Ermelo; and please, please to overlook this unfortunate incident and not call the police because it would ruin a charity mission. Somehow it worked, but it was expensive.

Next day Colonel Hoare arrived from Pietermaritzburg, driving a truck loaded with the special suitcases that had been prepared, each with an AK-47 and two magazines of ammunition in the false bottom. Each member of the group took possession of his. Nobody checked the bags as the bus went through the border post into Swaziland. But then another hiccup. When the bus arrived at the airport, Swazi porters began offloading the luggage. One took three bags in each hand – then failed to lift them they were so heavy. Horrified, Duffy yelled to the Frothblowers to each of them take his own bag, which they did. The porters did not put two and two together, but it had been another unanticipated close call. If the Swazi airport authorities had been alerted to there being something peculiar about the Frothblowers' luggage, the game would have been up.

The party boarded the Fokker Friendship, Colonel Hoare in command. It was a normal scheduled flight with a few other passengers. The Frothblowers played their role of boys on the spree with gusto. The aircraft took off for the Seychelles, via the Comores islands. Destination: a tropical island paradise. Surely the strangest invasion ever.

THINGS GO WRONG

All was going according to plan. The Air Swaziland Fokker Friendship had landed without incident about midday. The Frothblowers had been through immigration without any problem. Now it was customs, and they passed in loose groups through the "nothing to declare" green gate. Their bags were already being stacked on mini-buses outside the terminal building, in batches depending which hotel they were booked for. The few passengers who were not part of the Frothblowers' mission also made their way through.

One was a Seychellois Creole who had boarded in the Comores. He was returning from a holiday, resplendent in cream linen slacks and brightly coloured shirt. He seemed pretty pleased with himself. One of the customs officers signalled him to open his bag. The man protested, then complied. Reaching in, the customs officer pulled out a bunch of litchis, a tropical fruit the passenger had bought in the Comores but which it was illegal to bring into the Seychelles for reasons of plant disease control. The exchange between the passenger and the customs officer became heated. The customs man produced a copy of the regulations and began preparing some kind of document for a fine. The Seychellois exploded with rage.

"You do this to me because I am a Creole! You don't do it to these other people!" He indicated the Frothblowers who were filing through.

At which another customs officer stopped Johan Fritz and asked him to open his bag. Duffy was next in line and went cold. Reaching into his own bag, he pulled out a rubber bathtub duck and squeaked it at the customs officer, hoping to distract him and disarm him. The officer ignored it as he felt around in the bag and found it obviously had a false bottom. He began pulling the bag apart. Duffy ran to the exit to where the bags were being piled on the minibuses.

"Get the bags down! I think we've been rumbled!"

He ran back, to see a customs officer rushing out of an office with an AK-47 with a wooden butt. The Frothblowers were all of them pulling out their weapons by now, clipping in the ammunition. All hell broke loose as they opened up and the customs officer with the rifle went down, wounded though not fatally. Duffy dived for cover as the shooting broke out. Beside him Fritz dropped stone dead, shot through the heart by a stray bullet from one of his own men. The firing quietened. The Frothblowers fanned out and took control of the entire terminal, which was barely defended. Seychellois airport staff were herded together and told to sit tight. Two Frothblowers went into the control tower and took over. The airport was secure but the danger came from the military barracks, not far away near the end of the airport runway, which were known to contain about two hundred Tanzanian troops. The alarm would certainly have been raised by now, by radio or telephone.

All this threatened disaster. The plan had been for the Frothblowers to infiltrate, settle in and only days later give cutting-edge support when the Seychellois themselves went into rebellion. Hoare decided on an immediate attack on the barracks, to seize the armoury and hopefully neutralise the Tanzanians as a force. The advance party had come to the airport as incognito back-up, and when things went wrong Hoare ordered them into the mini-moke tourist vehicles they had brought with them for a full frontal attack on the barracks, the sooner the better. They set off and a brisk exchange of fire ensued at the gates of the barracks. But a nasty surprise lay in store. None of the advance party had noticed a 7.62mm anti-aircraft gun mounted just inside the barracks perimeter and this opened up on them to terrifying effect. They had to fall back for cover in the surrounding bush and Aubrey Brookes, a special forces man originally from Rhodesia, was badly wounded in the thigh. (He lost contact with his comrades and was eventually captured by the Seychellois).

The afternoon wore on. The light began to fail. The Frothblowers were in the stickiest of situations. They had the airport but nothing else. The well-armed Tanzanian force and the Seychellois army would soon move in. As darkness fell an armoured vehicle trundled down the road toward the terminal building. But the Frothblowers had anticipated such a thing and had strung a roadblock of civilian vehicles across the road. The armoured car's occupants tried to smash their way through, to ride across the blockage but ended up seesawing on top of it, unable to move forward or backward or train the machinegun. At least that threat was neutralised. Then mortars began to whistle and crunch about the airfield, coming from the direction of the army barracks. Vehicles were moving on the airfield and the terminal and control tower came under sporadic fire. The

Air Swaziland De Havilland, still parked there, was riddled with bullets and shrapnel, though it never caught fire.

Then another heavy vehicle was heard on the approach road. It turned out to be an armoured car, this time approaching just off-road. But it fared no better than the first. Its wheels started spinning in the soft sand, it was on its chassis, unable to move forward or back. The Frothblowers surrounded it. They slapped mud over its periscope, stood on top and rapped on the closed turret.

"Come out with your hands up!" They said it in English, French and Swahili. There was no response. "Come out or we'll burn you out with petrol!" Still no response.

A bottle was found and filled with petrol. An improvised wick was inserted. The Molotov cocktail. They repeated the warning, rapping on the turret. There was still no response. "Right," said Duffy. "Somebody give me a light."

But nobody in the group smoked. Nobody had matches or a lighter. They rapped on the turret again. "Hang on a bit. We're going to fetch some matches."

If there was a vestige of grim humour in this situation, it evaporated when the matches were brought. The Molotov cocktail was flung at the armoured car, which was instantly enveloped in flame. It was burning inside as well, as the petrol seeped in and next thing the hatch burst open and an armed Tanzanian appeared and was cut down by automatic fire before he had the chance to even aim his weapon. Then two Seychellois came out slowly, hands in the air. They were terrified.

Duffy had them marched to the area of the terminal where Hoare had set up command HQ. They were interrogated at length, through an interpreter, as to the disposition of the Tanzanian troops, their numbers and their armaments. The Frothblowers still hoped to fight their way out of this one, igniting the rebellion which they had come to support. Eventually Hoare was satisfied that his prisoners had told him all they could.

"Thank you," he said. "You may go now."

"Go?" They were absolutely astonished.

"Yes, go home. Tell everyone we are not here to attack the Seychellois people, we are here to liberate them."

Unable to believe their luck, the two prisoners ran off into the night. The mortar fire and heavy machinegun fire were building up. Frontal attack seemed imminent. The Frothblowers were indeed in a sticky situation.

In the control tower, Vernon Prinsloo, an ex-Rhodesian who had been national light-heavyweight boxing champion, sat with the Seychellois flight controller as mortar shell bursts and gunfire punctuated the night about the airfield. The controller had a serious attack of the jitters and spent much of the time beneath his desk. Then suddenly the radio crackled into life. It was an Air India flight from Harare, Zimbabwe, bound for Bombay, seeking permission to land. Mahe was a refuelling stop. This raised a moral problem. The aircraft could hardly be encouraged to land in the midst of a battle for control of the airport. Yet Prinsloo could not be totally explicit about the problem; it would have been radioed instantly about the world and the counter-coup attempt – already severely compromised – would be condemned internationally. Prinsloo advised against landing. The Air India flight should go on to Mauritius instead.

Then the Air India captain did something Duffy and his companions find puzzling to this day. He put the aircraft into a holding pattern for a good 50 minutes, burning up fuel while he discussed the position with the control tower, until eventually he had no option other than to land. Meanwhile, the Tanzanians and Seychellois army naturally presumed the mystery aircraft to be carrying reinforcements for the invaders and were ready to shoot at it with everything they had. In fact the aircraft carried civilians, including several VIPs in the Zimbabwean government, who were no doubt alarmed by the delay in landing but had no idea quite how precarious their position was. Nor did the Air India captain, Irmish Saxena – or Colonel Hoare and the Frothblowers for that matter – know that at least one truck was standing on the runway.

Captain Saxena decided to land. As he approached, the Tanzanians did have the decency to fire two red flares, warning him to abort. But he came in anyway, tracers arcing wildly but inaccurately after his aircraft as it touched down in the night. There was a sickening bang as a parked truck caught a trim baffle near the undercarriage and tore it off, but the lurching aircraft managed to stay on course and slow, the engines screeching in reverse thrust. Three feet closer to the undercarriage and the aircraft would certainly have cartwheeled, killing everyone on board.

As Colonel Hoare watched from the terminal, he said to Duffy: "If anything happens to that plane, we'll get the blame." But the gods were on the side of the passengers and aircrew. The Boeing

707 taxied into position, engines still screaming, and one of the Frothblowers drove Duffy out to it on the mobile gangway. A door opened and a figure appeared. Duffy was at the top of the steps, his AK-47 slung over his shoulder.

"Are you the captain?" He had to cup his hands and yell above the still-screaming engines.

"I'm the first officer."

"I need to speak to the captain."

"Come in."

Duffy was led to the flight deck where he was introduced to Saxena. He explained the situation. The Air India flight had flown into an attempted counter-coup. Control of the airport was still being contested. Saxena, who had once been an officer in the Indian Air Force, asked if he could meet Hoare. He, the first officer and the navigator were driven to the terminal.

"Why did you land the aircraft?" Hoare asked as they were introduced. He never did get a satisfactory answer. They discussed the options, which were precious few. Saxena said he wanted to leave first thing next morning after refuelling. But the mortar barrage was intensifying. He changed his mind. He would refuel right away and take off as soon as possible.

But how could he take a passenger aircraft through the hell of tracer bullets and shrapnel that was developing outside? Could a cease-fire be negotiated? Dozens of Seychellois airport officials were still there under guard, and somebody was found to telephone the presidency and put Captain Saxena on the line. An astonishing dialogue followed between President Albert Rene and Saxena, who explained that this was a civilian flight that carried some senior

Zimbabwean political figures. It had absolutely no connection with the coup attempt, of which he had only just been informed. Rene considered and hedged. Then he agreed to order the troops to cease hostilities until the Air India flight had taken off. But this should happen as soon as possible. And, he insisted, nobody else should be taken. Saxena agreed.

The barrage went quiet. Duffy got hold of two Seychellois airport operatives to set up the complicated refuelling process. He drove them out to the fuel tanks for the first step in the operation, using an airport runabout vehicle but with the lights switched off just in case, leaning out and shining the way with a torch. But all remained quiet. The fuel line was connected up to the Boeing's tanks and the fuel started pumping. Duffy got into conversation with the two technicians, who were friendly and totally co-operative. He got the impression they rather approved of any attempt to oust Rene. The tanks were now full. One of the technicians thrust a requisition book at him.

"Can you sign for the fuel, please?"

"Oh, certainly." Duffy signed with a flourish: "Lieutenant-General Mickey Mouse."

Elsewhere, Captain Saxena and his officers had been busy. They took a drive down the runway to make sure it was clear. They dragged out of the way the truck that had torn off the stabiliser trim. The Tanzanians were observing the truce. The aircraft was now ready to fly. The stabiliser trim was not essential to take-off and flight.

Back in the terminal, Saxena spoke to Hoare. "I don't want to know how many men are in your group. That's your business. But I can carry an extra 50 passengers."

This was a way out. Hoare and Duffy considered. But the flight was to Bombay. South Africa at that stage had no diplomatic relations with India because of apartheid. Many of the Frothblowers were former Rhodesian special forces and current South African special forces personnel. They had South African travel documents. They would not be welcome in Bombay. South Africa was another option, in spite of the lack of diplomatic relations. Saxena agreed to fly them there.

This is, of course, Duffy's account of what happened. In the subsequent air piracy trial the Natal Supreme Court was to take a different view: that the aircraft had been diverted to Durban under duress. Duffy is adamant that no weapon was ever pointed at anyone; no threat was ever made. Saxena made the offer out of humanitarian recognition of the Frothblowers' predicament. In Duffy's support, one of Saxena's officers did tell a radio station that the incident had been not so much a "hijacking" as a "commandeering" (though a court of law would probably see no distinction). Saxena and Duffy are firm friends to this day. Duffy flew to India (at great personal risk) to support and promote Saxena when he wrote his own account of the incident. Every Christmas he gets a telephone call from Saxena. Every Diwali Saxena gets a telephone call from him. Could it be that (perfectly understandable) international strictures against air piracy in this case overrode some human sympathy and decency?

Whatever the case, about 1 am next morning the Air India flight took off, the body of Johan Fritz in the cargo hold, the Frothblowers' weapons tied up on the floor in a blanket. The Tanzanians held their fire, yet at one stage Duffy thought he heard the sound of bullets slapping the fuselage. But it was only the Frothblowers exultantly giving the parabat clap; many passengers joined in, relieved to be out of it. Drinks were served; the stewardesses refused payment. During the flight, a blonde girl from Zimbabwe and one of the mercenaries struck up such a rapport that they ended up joining the mile-high club. If this was a hijacking, it was a most strange one.

19

THE HIJACKERS LAND

The Air India Boeing touched down at Louis Botha Airport, Durban, in the predawn darkness. A reception committee was waiting: the airport police plus a company from the Reconaissance Battalion based on the Bluff, the headland overlooking the entrance to Durban harbour. Ironically enough – though neither side was to know it at the time – they were of the same special forces component of the South African Defence Force as so many of the Frothblowers party. A transponder activated by Captain Saxena had notified air traffic control in Durban that the flight was being made under duress.

On the flight, Colonel Hoare and Duffy had discussed their options. Under the impression that the Seychelles expedition had been virtually on behalf of the South African government, which would co-operate in spite of the failure and hush the thing up, it seemed important that the identity of the force should be kept secret, so its members could be allowed to simply melt back into society. To keep away from the public spotlight, Duffy told Captain Saxena to taxi the Boeing away from the normal strip of apron for arrivals, down towards the air force base at the northern end of the runway. The idea was that he should negotiate with the authorities to allow the group's members to disembark unobtrusively and disappear. Failing that, he could argue for another aircraft to be made available, with parachutes for the entire party. It could take off and drop them somewhere over the Natal hinterland, from which they could make their own way home. Given the likely international repercussions, it was important that the identity of those involved in the failed counter-coup should remain secret.

As mentioned elsewhere, Duffy had become a well-known figure in Durban, either running up and down the rugby touchlines at King's Park with his camera or taking social shots of Durban nightlife. Security forces fanned around the Boeing as it came to a halt, automatic rifles trained. A jeep sped out from the airport building. In it was a certain Colonel Mouton, commander of the police at Louis Botha. He came up the steps which had been pushed into place, ready to confront the highjackers.

"My God, Duffy!" he exclaimed as he came through the doorway. "What are you doing here?" Colonel Mouton was a rugby enthusiast and recognised Duffy from King's Park. So much for anonymity.

Duffy undertook the negotiating. It was not as easy as he and Hoare had anticipated. There were international complications; a foreign aircraft had at the very least been unlawfully commandeered, possibly hijacked. The foreign country in question had a hostile relationship with the South African government of those days. There were the strictest international conventions against air piracy, to which South Africa was signatory. A nod and a wink was difficult.

The sun rose. A knot of press photographers were gathered on the airport tarmac, kept at a distance by the security police. Laurie

Bloomfield, chief photographer of the Daily News – a newspaper from the same stable as the Sunday Tribune – looked at the scene through his tele-lens. To his astonishment, there in the doorway of the Boeing, at the top of the steps, stood his photographer colleague Peter Duffy, expostulating and arguing with the police.

He called a security policeman: "I want to go on board the plane."

"You can't."

"Why not? The Sunday Tribune are there already."

"What?" The security policeman almost fainted.

And so it dragged on. The Air India passengers were allowed to disembark, even though almost none of them had travel documents valid for South Africa, the international outcast. So were the flight and cabin crew. Eventually the mercenary group were allowed off the aircraft and transferred to a military Hercules transport which flew them all the way to Waterkloof air force base, in Pretoria. From there they were taken to Sonderwater prison, also in Pretoria, where they were detained under South Africa's draconian security legislation – which provided for indefinite detention incommunicado without trial – to be interviewed by senior security personnel.

The full anomaly of the situation at first escaped Duffy and his companions. Many of the group had backgrounds with the former Rhodesian or the current South African special forces. Raids into neighbouring states had been part of their military experience as first Rhodesia, then South Africa, struck across the borders at the forces that threatened the status quo. It was considered legitimate, a familiar military tactic. The sortie to the Seychelles seemed in much the same category, although only semi-official. The government knew all about it, they had been assured. They were under the impression they were at Sonderwater for some kind of debriefing. Early official reaction from South Africa's Minister of Police, Louis le Grange, encouraged them in this belief. All they appeared to have done, Le Grange declared, was "run around in the bush and shoot out a few windows." Boys will be boys, after all. The group made a full statement of the facts as they recalled. They had no idea their statements would eventually form the basis of a criminal prosecution.

Conflicting statements issued from government sources. The United States, Britain and other western countries were putting heavy pressure on the South African government to act with firmness. The slightest sign of concession to the group who had commandeered the Air India flight could lose South African Airways its landing rights all over the world. Days went by. Then it was announced that most of the group would be released unconditionally. Five, including Hoare and Duffy, would be charged with "man-stealing" (a clumsily over-literal translation of the Afrikaans term for abduction) and would appear before a Pretoria magistrate. This duly happened and they were remanded for a month on bail of R10, 000 in Hoare's case and R5,000 each for the others.

More time passed and International pressure intensified. And then the pendulum swung. Hoare, Duffy, and the other three charged with "man-stealing" were arrested and charged under the Civil Aviation Offences Act, of 1972 (a virtual replication of similar legislation against air piracy that had been enacted world-wide). So were the members of the group who had previously been discharged. The "man-stealing" charges were dropped. Bail was set at R20,000 for Hoare, R10,000 each for Duffy and the three others and R1,000 for the remaining thirty-five. The trial was set down for March 10 in the Natal Supreme Court, in the provincial capital, Pietermaritzburg. There had been a complete reversal. The South African authorities were now throwing the book at Hoare and his men.

ON TRIAL

The College Road Supreme Court in Pietermaritzburg is a venerable pile of red-brick Victorian architecture that had been, during the colonial era, the Natal Native High Court. As this court frequently tried cases involving factional warfare among the Zulu clans, one of its features was a large dock built to accommodate entire war parties. However, even this was not enough to accommodate the 42 men of the Seychelles group. A special mini-grandstand of scaffolding and planking had been erected at the rear of the courtroom to accommodate all of them. The College Road courthouse swarmed with television crews and journalists from around the world. The normally somnolent Natal capital had never before known such a flurry of attention.

The trial was to drag on for more than five months, as the prosecution produced evidence from the police and security services who had handled the Air India flight's arrival in Durban; from the statements taken from the group at Sonderwater prison; and evidence given on commission in the Seychelles by the Air India flight captain and his flight crew. (These had not been allowed by their government to appear in person at the trial because of the lack of diplomatic recognition between India and South Africa at the time).

Colonel Hoare himself took a lively interest in proceedings and was to spend four days in the witness box under examnination and cross-examination. He was eventually to represent himself, and the men he had commanded, as funding for legal representation ran out. But for most of the group the legal proceedings meant complete boredom, with only the occasional blip of excitement. One such was when one of the mercenaries took exception to being filmed as they filed into the courthouse and shoved the cameraman's lens so hard that the eyepiece jammed back into his eye, giving him a shiner. This cameraman then laid a charge of assault which, after air piracy, was pretty small beer. On another occasion somebody discovered that several of the mercenaries were "packing heat", as the expression goes. They were sitting there in a court of law with firearms in their shoulder holsters. It caused a flurry and the introduction of a metal detector so that the accused could be scanned for firearms every day as they arrived, but this led only to a further flurry when, one morning, the policeman responsible discovered that his metal detector had disappeared. The poor man was in some distress, so the mercenaries took pity and told him in which fire bucket they had hidden it. But such diversions were only occasional. For the most part the men were bored stiff and they passed their time in the dock surreptitiously reading and doodling in jotters.

Duffy had several of the group staying with him in the Spook House in Durban. While the trial was on, they would drive up to

Pietermaritzburg every day. At weekends and during court recesses, time could hang a little heavy.

For five months and more it went on. The case was heard on the very narrow issue of whether or not Hoare, Duffy and the others had contravened sections of the Civil Aviation Act relating to interfering with an aircraft in flight; having in their possession while an aircraft was in flight arms and ammunition; and interfering with good order, procedures and discipline at airports. (The Act does not use the express terms "air piracy" or "hijacking"). The court did not concern itself with the rights or wrongs of the attempted counter-coup on the Seychelles and the shoot-out at Mahe airport; nor did it address the issue of whether or not the South African government had backed the attempt. It wanted to know whether the fact that the Air India flight was boarded (by Duffy) before its doors had been opened for passengers to disembark meant that technically it was still in flight; whether Duffy's presence on the flight deck with an AK-47 slung on his shoulder constituted "interference"; Whether the presence of either Charles Goatley or Tullio Moneta on the flight deck in a monitoring capacity during the flight to Durban constituted "interference"; and whether the mercenaries had interfered with order and procedures by getting the aircraft refuelled in Mahe and then directing it to park in an out-of-the-way spot in Durban.

Looked at purely technically, Hoare and his men clearly had some difficulty here, however cordial the relationship with the Air India command and crew might ultimately have worked out to be. But it got worse. Giving evidence on commission in the Seychelles, Captain Saxena flatly contradicted Hoare's version that he had offered to take the mercenary party on board in gratitude for their arranging a ceasefire to allow take-off. Although in his statement to the South African Police on arrival in Durban Saxena had made no mention of being coerced into taking the group on board and flying them to Durban, on the Seychelles he denied in evidence heard on commission that he had offered to fly Hoare out with him. In fact he quoted Hoare saying: "If you follow our instructions, you will not be harmed. You try to double-cross us, we will shoot one of you and blow up the aircraft." (Something Hoare vehemently denied).

It was Saxena's word against Hoare's. The court accepted Saxena's version. In his summing up, Justice Neville James, Acting Judge President of Natal, had this to say:

"If the accuseds' conduct can be properly described as a hijack in the popular sense, it was a most unusual one. It was not a planned hijack specifically embarked upon to escape from an oppressive regime or to advance some political or sociological theory, or to exact some political or financial advantage by taking hostages. The accuseds' conduct in getting onto the plane and persuading the captain to fly them to Durban was not part of a long term plan but arose as a result of the providential arrival of the Air India plane on a routine flight at a time when the accused were in a perilous situation of their own creation when their plan to take over the Seychelles by force of arms was in serious danger of collapse. During the flight they had no reason to treat the members of the crew or the passengers impolitely or uncivilly. This was wholly unnecessary as long as their decision to fly to Durban was respected, and very little can be made out of the fact that the accused behaved well on the plane.

"The Court is left with an overwhelming impression that once Saxena fell under his control Hoare gradually put the pressure on him and by stages manoeuvred him into a position where he was obliged to fly them to Durban. The Court has no doubt that Saxena never voluntarily agreed to take the accused to Durban, that there was no firm agreement on the lines stated by Hoare and that Saxena had no choice in the matter."

That nailed it down. On Count 1 – seizing and exercising control over the aircraft – Hoare, Duffy, Moneta and Doorewaard were found guilty, along with the remainder of the accused. On Count 2 – jeopardising the safety of Mahe airport – Hoare, Moneta and Doorewaard were found guilty. On Count 3 – jeopardising the safety of Louis Botha airport (Durban) – Hoare and Duffy were found guilty. On Count 4 – possession of arms on the aircraft – all were acquitted.

Hoare was sentenced to ten years' imprisonment on Count one and five years each on Counts 2 and 3, to run concurrently – an effective fifteen years. Duffy, Moneta and Doorewaard were given five years each; three others were sentenced to twenty months, one to ten months and the remainder to six months which, with normal remission for good behaviour, meant an effective four months. Charlie Dukes, an American, was found not guilty on all counts and discharged. The rest were taken from the courthouse to Pietermaritzburg New Prison. Those with the lighter sentences were transported next morning to Diepkloof prison, in the

Transsvaal. Hoare, Duffy, Moneta and Doorewaard had applied for leave to appeal against conviction and sentence and stayed on in Pietermaritzburg. When word arrived that leave to appeal had been refused, they were bundled into a one-ton truck and driven to Pretoria Central prison. The door had clanged shut resoundingly on the Frothblowers expedition.

PRETORIA CENTRAL PRISON

As the Seychelles group waited for sentencing, Duffy did his homework on prison life, reading up what he could about the routines, speaking to a couple of old lags of his acquaintance. It seemed that one of the key instruments in the jailers' asserting of authority was control over time. None of the inmates ever knew what time it was, not until the siren for a meal sounded. Wristwatches or clocks of any sort were forbidden. No prisoner was aware at any time of day or night what the time actually was, it was dictated by the comings and goings, the cursings and cajoling of the warders. It was an important psychological instrument in getting docility and obedience from the prisoners.

The day before sentence was to be handed down in the College Road courthouse, Duffy went to a Pietermaritzburg jeweller's shop and bought the tiniest lady's wrist watch he could find. He removed the strap and secreted it on his person (decency forbids inquiring too closely as to where). He was confident its whereabouts would escape the closest strip search which, he had been assured, every prisoner would undergo on admission. It was to stay with him, undetected, for the jail time that stretched ahead and to be not just a useful instrument in planning the minutiae of prison life but a psychological boost as well, affirmation of his human individuality, something which the prison system was designed to break down.

Pretoria Central Prison is a frowning stone pile, built early in the last century in full conformity with the punitive ethos of the time. Prisoners slept on thin mats on the stone floor, sometimes three to a cell. The food was meagre and unappetising. The warders – known to all inmates, of whatever ethnic origin, as the "Boere" – were almost all of them Afrikaners who specialised in torrents of abuse screamed in their own language, whether it was understood or not. The warders were not socially out of the top drawer. In any service a quota of psychopathic bullies is statistically likely to be present, and the South African prison service was no different. Colonel Hoare and Duffy were to witness brutal birchings that drew blood. Pretoria Central was, notoriously, the place where all South Africa's executions by hanging were conducted and, in the apartheid era, there was a weekly quota. In the dysfunctional human wastelands that developed and festered over the years, communities had grown up living by a kind of law of the jungle where criminality was a way of life, and life itself was cheap. It resulted in a regular quota of hangings as the law took its retributive course, this eventually being augmented by "political" executions as revolutionary activity began to take hold. The prisons were still racially segregated in those days. Hoare, Duffy and their companions were aware of the weekly horror being conducted in the execution block as the entire prison reverberated with song and hymns from the black cell blocks as they waited for the fall of the multiple trapdoors, greeting it with a resounding "Hallelujah!". Then silence. It was an eeriness to which one could never get accustomed. And then the week would continue with its round of dreariness and slothful activity, all within the prison atmosphere of sweat, despair and sheer hopelessness. It was something designed to break the human spirit. It was light years away from Hoare's background in the officer corps of the British army; from Duffy's privileged upbringing in Scotland and London.

Duffy was particularly concerned about Hoare who, at his advanced age, suddenly found himself living this nightmare. He realised that to survive prison life you had to make small, incremental advances. He had already outfoxed the system in a small way by smuggling in his wristwatch. Other advances were needed to make life slightly more bearable, even if only in the psychological sense. Hoare was given a "soft" detail as an orderly in the prison's hospital section. (For all its harshness, the prisons service was meticulous about caring for the health of inmates). It might have been in recognition of his age. It might even have been a kind of grudging admission that the "crime" for which he had been sent to jail was something not of his own making. Whatever the reason, it was an advance, the kind of thing that gave you hope.

Duffy was allowed one prison visit a month. Looking at him through the thick glass of the vestibule, a warder present to listen to every word of their conversation then cut it short when time was up, was Georgia, his partner. She had come up from Durban and was looking wonderful. But they could not touch or pass any kind of message. Duffy held up a piece of paper against the glass, then quickly took it away again. The Boere warder had not noticed. Scrawled on the piece of paper had been the words: "Tell Victor to write to me."

Victor Janssen was the owner of *La Popote* restaurant in Durban, which specialised in French cuisine and the finest of fine wines. Duffy had been a regular there, photographing the clientele chatting to the chefs, often himself working in the kitchen. He had a flair for the gastronomic arts and considered himself part of the *La Popote* operation.

A few weeks later, Duffy was told the prison commandant wished to see him. He was marched into the commandant's office. The first thing he noticed was the letter that sat on the desk in front of the commandant. It had the *La Popote* letterhead. Every letter received by a prisoner is read first by the prison authorities.

"Duffy," the commandant said sternly, "You are a cook?"

"Yes sir."

Janssen had apparently sent an effusive letter: "Ah, Peter, when are you coming out? Our customers are wanting you, they say only you can make the sauces they want … "

"Why didn't you tell us you was a cook?"

"I didn't think it was important, sir."

"Everything is important, Duffy. We have to know everything about you."

At which, as though inflicting heavy punishment for his transgressions, the commandant ordered that Duffy should forthwith work in the kitchen for the officers' mess. If he was in demand by the discerning gourmands of *La Popote*, why should the officers of Pretoria Central Prison be denied?

This was a significant advance against the system. Not only did Duffy suddenly have a status that was close to privileged, he had access to food of an entirely different quality. He fast developed smuggling techniques that allowed him to keep Hoare supplied with delicacies in the privacy of his cell that made prison life almost bearable. The psychological lift for both was immense.

***

In prison you seize on any opportunity, anything out of the ordinary that could relieve the tedium. Pretoria Central has a great hallway as you come in off the street through the massive solid doors under a Gothic arch, then through another huge metal door. This hall is like a Victorian railway station, a massive glass-paned dome supported by steel girders. Underneath, prisoners shuffle about the expanse of already highly polished stone floor on rags, polishing and repolishing in morose silence. It is part of the brute pointlessness of prison life.

Duffy was on an errand one day when he noticed something lying on the highly polished surface. They were thin strips of putty, scattered across various parts of the floor. Workmen high above had been repairing parts of the roof where the glass panes had become loose as their holding putty dried and crumbled after more than a century of exposure to the elements. The workmen were putting in new putty. As they scraped away the residue for neatness, as glaziers do, small strips of wet putty fell down below. Duffy moved about the floor like a ferret, picking up the strips of putty, rolling them into a ball and hiding it on his person. You never knew when this might come in useful.

In the end the putty that Duffy collected came to have a recreational/therapeutic and artistic value. Fiddling with it alone in his cell, he discovered in himself a talent to model small figurines – "mannetjies" (little men) as the prison population came to know them – of amusing and artistic appeal. They were like miniature garden gnomes in a range of poses and attitudes. Dried out, they could be painted and became attractive decorations. They took on a definite exchange value – you could swap a mannetjie for all kinds of small treats – tobacco, sweets, food. The warders also cottoned on to the trade. Their wives expressed interest in the mannetjies as home decorations, and Duffy would find putty rolled up and squeezing through the peephole to his cell like an emerging turd as the warder in the corridor outside supplied the raw material for still more mannetjies.

It was a harmless enough craze but the prison authorities took a dim view. Prison was not a place for hobbies, fun and collectors' items, it was a place of punishment. Mannetjies were verboten. A blitz was ordered. Cells were searched and mannetjies confiscated. Putty became a banned substance. Gradually the mannetjies disappeared from circulation, the demand dried up and Duffy had to find something else to occupy his time. But it had been the kind of interlude that chalked up another small victory against the system; the more so when, one day, Duffy had occasion to visit the office of one of the senior warders. This office had confiscated mannetjies decorating every available flat area of space – the warder's desk, windowsills, pelmet tops and bookcase. Recognition is welcome. It was another of those incremental gains that made prison life slightly less intolerable.

***

As outlined elsewhere, the Durban July Handicap – Africa's premier horserace – had always loomed large in Duffy's life. This annual extravaganza of racing colours, wealth and outrageous fashion in the crisp winter's air of Durban on the first Saturday in July not only attracted him for its photographic opportunities – he had become expert at getting the definitive shot at the winning post – but had become part of his calendar, from the racing itself, to the tipsy ladies flashing all, to the Thirteenth Race when, in the half-dark, male streakers set off down the main straight in front of the grandstand. The July was for Duffy an occasion for which he yearned and pined from his incarceration in Pretoria Central.

It was late in June when he discovered a strange rash on one foot. It was fairly minor, but an idea began to take hold. He filled his gumboots with water and went sloshing about in them for a day. When he took the boots off that evening, the rash had become positively virulent. He reported at sick bay next morning. The health of the inmates was one thing the prison authorities did take seriously. He was given a lotion, which he disposed of in one of the kitchen rubbish bins. He again filled his boots with water. The following day the rash was alarming in appearance and had spread to both feet. This was the kind of thing that could spread through the entire prison. Quarantine was required, the prison medics decided. Duffy needed to go into hospital, under guard.

Duffy knew that the hospital always chosen for such emergencies was HF Verwoerd, in Pretoria. He would be admitted to a private ward, shackled to his bed and a warder would watch over him 24 hours a day. But he also knew that each private ward at HF Verwoerd had a television screen on the wall. He would be able to watch the Durban July.

The young doctor who examined him on arrival at HF Verwoerd seemed a little puzzled. Duffy sensed that he was not convinced by the prison medics' diagnosis.

Then he said straight out: "How did this really happen?" He seemed not hostile, almost sympathetic. Duffy sensed that this was a time for candour.

"Well, I had this rash. Then I made it worse by putting water in my boots for two days."

"So you wanted to come to hospital?"

"Yes, I want to watch the July Handicap on TV."

"How long do you have to be here?"

"About 10 days."

"I'll fix it."

So it was that Duffy ended up ensconced in the warmth and comfort of a hospital bed with a large television screen on the wall opposite, the only minor discomfort being that he was shackled to the bed frame by one leg and was being watched constantly by a Boere seated in a chair at the end of his bed. This Boere would be relieved by a colleague every couple of hours, they took it in spells. If Duffy had reason to answer a call of nature, the Boere would unshackle him and accompany him to the lavatories, waiting for him immediately outside his cubicle. There was no chance whatever of Duffy making a break for it. His trips to the lavatories were occasioned partly by calls of nature, partly by the need to flush away the anti-inflammatory pills that had been prescribed with a straight face by the young doctor. Duffy had no intention of having the rash clear up before the July Handicap was run.

The days were counting down to the first Saturday in July. Duffy was relaxing in bed with a magazine when two acquaintances arrived in the ward. They had gone to Pretoria Central requesting to visit Duffy. Told that he was in HF Verwoerd hospital, they drove on there. A visit was a visit whether in jail or hospital. But on their way they stopped off and bought a bottle of brandy. Hospitals were less fussy about gifts than prisons

The Boere was astounded when the two visitors suddenly appeared. He leaped to his feet to shoo them out, expostulating that this was a prison site, they were not allowed to visit. In the confusion one of them managed to slip the bottle of brandy under Duffy's pillow.

Duffy drank a lot of coffee that night. The Boere seemed not to notice that his cup never emptied. He was not to see the brandy bottle that was steadily emptying. Duffy had been inside for more than a year by this stage. During that time alcohol had not passed his lips. This was glorious. At one stage he fell out of bed, held in only by the shackled leg. The anti-inflammatory pills spilled out of his pyjama jacket all over the floor. The Boere seemed to have fallen asleep. Befuddled and laughing to himself, Duffy groped about on the floor and recovered most if not all of the tablets he was supposed to be taking. Next morning he felt only slightly the worse for wear and anyway had the whole day to sleep it off. The rest of the brandy he hid in his bedside locker, saving it for July Handicap day, when he had another secret celebration. Seldom has any television viewer participated with such fervour at a distance in the events at Greyville racecourse on July day. This was most certainly a significant triumph over the system. Duffy's morale was high.

***

Duffy had served 21 months of his five-year sentence and was approaching that point at which he could be considered for early release on parole as a prisoner of good behaviour, when both he and Hoare were informed, absolutely unexpectedly, that they were to be transferred back to New Prison, Pietermaritzburg. This was welcome news. New Prison was, as the name suggested, a leap toward modern values. The prisoners slept on bunks, not on the floor as in Pretoria Central. Visits by family and friends would be very much easier. And they had noticed, even during their earlier brief incarceration in Pietermaritzburg, that the prison service there was considerably more anglicised in its ways and its values than in Pretoria.

Duffy was sent to the mess kitchen for duties, Hoare to the jail's petrol pumps. But after only two weeks of this new jail existence, Duffy was called to the commandant's office and told he was being released on parole to work at *La Popote* restaurant, in Durban. He was to leave in an hour. He was back in his civilian clothes when he found the colonel at the pumps and broke the glad news to him. Duffy felt bad about abandoning Hoare, yet at the same time believed the current course of events would soon see the colonel's release as well, in spite of the length of time he was still supposed to serve.

Hoare himself pays tribute (in his own book, *The Seychelles Affair*) to Duffy's supportive role during their time in jail. "He had been with me every step of the way and, as I told him then, he had been a son, a brother and a friend to me. No man could wish for a more loyal companion."

Released from prison, Duffy plunged with gusto into his old life in Durban, this time as a chef at *La Popote* until eventually he moved back into his old job as a photographer at the Sunday Tribune, which welcomed him with open arms. Christmas 1984 was approaching. Rumours began to circulate that Hoare himself was about to be released early. These were based partly on an amnesty for prisoners declared to coincide with Prime Minister PW Botha's merging of the posts of prime minister and state president in his own person; partly on the words of a senior prisons department officer to Hoare he had been recommended for release, on grounds of age plus good behaviour, in January. A photograph appeared in one of the newspapers of Duffy in full chef's outfit, basting a goose at *La Popote* in anticipation of his colonel's release. In fact Duffy had also arranged for an open Rolls Royce to be hired so that Hoare could be driven in triumph from the prison in Pietermaritzburg to his home in Hilton. Whether all this really served to set back Hoare's case for early release is difficult to tell. The prisons service detests such publicity. But that does not explain the sudden reversal in fortunes for Hoare. Inexplicably he was put into solitary confinement for three months and his privileges were withdrawn. Hoare himself heard unsubstantiated rumours that the volcanically unpredictable PW Botha himself had been falsely told that Hoare had written a defamatory letter about him to President Mobutu, of Zaire. The weeks and months dragged by with Hoare sinking into ever-deeper despair until one morning in May he was informed that he was to be released at three o'clock that afternoon. Not even his wife had been informed and he was driven home to Hilton unannounced. The episode is still unexplained. If the prisons service was unimpressed by Duffy-style publicity, it had exacted a painful revenge. But at least the last and the most senior of the Seychelles group was free.

EARLY RELEASE

Duffy soon gravitated back to his old photographic job on the Sunday Tribune. When he left for the Seychelles he had put in for three weeks' leave, and this had been more than somewhat overstayed, but to his credit Tribune editor Ian Wyllie forgave him and took him on again. He missed Duffy's verve and professional can-do attitude. Wyllie was a man of liberal inclination, who had absolutely no sympathy for the gung-ho militarism of those who would have automatically supported the Seychelles expedition, but he was also a man who could sense where an injustice had been done. Duffy was back in harness. Again he charged up and down the rugby touchline at King's Park. Again he was about at all hours following photographic tip-offs from his old contacts in the police and elsewhere. Again he was the life and soul of the classier restaurants.

But it was a changing South Africa to which he returned. Much of his work now involved coverage of the volatile townships around Durban and other parts of KwaZulu-Natal, where the African National Congress and the traditional Zulu-based Inkatha Freedom Party were in a low-intensity civil war as they sought the loyalty and support of Natal's majority African population as apartheid and Afrikaner nationalism ran into crisis. They were trying and dangerous times for a photographer. But then came the political transition and the environment changed again. Diplomatic and open trade relations were re-established with countries such as India, which had been broken off decades earlier as the Nationalists introduced apartheid. Suddenly Air India was flying from Bombay to Durban, a link between India and the sizeable Asian population of Durban, with its ancestral, cultural and religious connections, along with significant business connections that had previously been via the back door.

Duffy happened to be at the airport when the first scheduled Air India flight arrived in Durban. At a small ceremony in the terminal an Air India manager spoke of the historic significance of this first Air India flight. Somebody gently reminded him that it was the first "scheduled" Air India flight; there had been an unscheduled one back in 1981. Duffy was taking the photographs. All sides took it in high good humour.

***

The ship's band was playing on the quarterdeck of the frigate, sitars and other Asian instruments among the brass and woodwind of the naval bands to which Durban had previously been accustomed; a curious amalgam of the traditions of the Royal Navy and of the Indian sub-continent. Three frigates and a corvette of the Indian navy were on a goodwill visit to Durban. The occasion was a cocktail party, guest of honour the Mayor of Durban and councillors. The western/eastern musical medley seemed to somehow capture Durban's status as a touching point of Asia, Africa and Europe.

Next thing a chunkily built photographer came marching up the gangplank to get social pictures.

"Ooh, it's Peter Duffy," squealed Latha Reddy, vivacious Indian consul-general in Durban. "I hope he doesn't steal our ship!"

At which the captain and his officers made a beeline for Duffy, posing with him for pictures, shaking his hand, slapping him on the back. His role in the Air India "hijacking" had spread far. Revulsion? Ostracism? Not a bit of it, Duffy was a celebrity. It was with some difficulty that he managed to break free from the attention and get the pictures of the mayor and the others that he had come for.

***

Yogin Devan, news editor of the Sunday Tribune, got wind that one of the air hostesses on the Air India flight that had been commandeered in the Seychelles would be on a flight to Durban. He set it up for her to meet Duffy again at a restaurant for lunch. He arranged with Air India for her to be collected from her hotel on the beachfront.

Normally a Sunday Tribune pool car would have done the job. But Duffy had other ideas. He would drive the car himself. He borrowed a peaked cap from one of the security staff at the newspaper building and set off for the beachfront as chauffeur.

He gave a sizzling salute as he handed the air hostess into the back seat of the car, then listened politely and attentively as she told him, as he drove across the city, how nervous she was about having to re-encounter the man who had taken her aircraft.

"Oh, a very dangerous man, ma'am," he agreed. Then he recounted a few imaginary atrocities for which, he said, Duffy was currently on trial. She became still more apprehensive.

"Don't worry, ma'am, stay close to me. I'll look after you."

He ushered her into the restaurant where Devan and some of his staff were at a table with two empty places. He saw her into her chair then sat down opposite and took off his chauffeur's cap. He held out his hand.

"Peter Duffy, my dear. So nice to make your acquaintance again."

***

It was twenty-five years since the abortive counter-coup. Much had changed. Communism had collapsed world-wide, the Cold War had ended. South Africa was a constitutional democracy. The Seychelles had scrapped its Marxist-style one-party system and adopted real democracy. Rene had this time been legitimately voted into power. Tourism from South Africa was significant in the Seychelles economy.

Many of those who participated in the Seychelles escapade were still around. Colonel Hoare was alternating his time between his sons in Durban and Cape Town, mainly writing books. Duffy was working as a high-profile press photographer, listening with quiet amusement to pub talk and dinner table talk where all kinds of heroes described their role in the Seychelles invasion; how they had held guns to the heads of the Air India flight crew. Some had even taken over the Boeing's controls. Duffy had, of course, never seen one of them in his life before. But even at the distance of a quarter-century, all kinds of people liked to claim a slice of the action.

Martin Dolinchek was still around. His was a curious story. BOSS had completely disowned him when the expedition went wrong; ended his salary, cut off his pension and left his family destitute while he was in jail on the Seychelles (where he had been captured as part of the advance party). Embittered and by now totally disillusioned about the apartheid government's cause, Dolinchek returned at a time apartheid was disintegrating anyway. He found himself on a farm in the far northern Transvaal, just beneath the Zimbabwe border. From there he crossed into Zimbabwe, sought out the African National Congress and offered them his services as a former BOSS operative. He must have been a valuable acquisition at first for the knowledge he brought with him, but Dolinchek was by now on the skids. He drank heavily, he had left his wife and children and he seemed to lead a marginal existence as some kind of apparatchik of the African National Congress. Probably he was doing much the same as he had for BOSS, though almost certainly nowhere near as effectively.

Much had changed, in the Seychelles and in South Africa, twenty-five years on. But an anniversary is an anniversary. The Seychelles government decided to mark the occasion when it had fought off an apartheid-backed coup. Various celebrations and ceremonies were held. Various people were invited from abroad. And among them were Dolinchek and Duffy.

Dolinchek was perhaps understandable. He had switched sides. He represented a fraternal government. But Duffy? He had merely gone back to his old existence. He had renounced nothing, embraced nothing, he was as apolitical as before. Yet he was invited. Again, he was in the arrivals hall at Mahe airport. But waiting to meet him this time was a tall Seychellois brigadier, possibly as nervously uncertain within himself as Duffy was about the encounter.

Duffy broke the ice: "Can you tell me where the lost property office is?"

"The lost property office?"

"Yes, I left my AK-47 here 25 years ago."

The brigadier's lips twitched then he went poker-faced again. But Duffy knew he had him. For a week Duffy was driven about the island by the brigadier. He ended up staying at his home. It could not have been more cordial. Later that same brigadier was to contact Duffy by telephone in Durban, setting him up as a sort of unofficial local agent in negotiations with a local shipyard for repairs to the one small vessel that comprised the Seychellois navy.

It had been not just a very strange sort of hijacking. It turned to have a very strange aftermath as well.

***

Duffy has maintained friendly contact with Captain Saxena, the Air India pilot, who is now retired and living in Bombay. As noted elsewhere, he telephones him every Diwali. Saxena returns the compliment every Christmas. But then Saxena contacted him to tell him he had written a book about the Air India affair. He invited Duffy to the launch in Bombay.

This was problematic. Duffy has a conviction for air piracy. Would he not be arrested as he tried to enter? Would the Indian authorities consider that justice had been done in Pietermaritzburg and Pretoria and let bygones be bygones? Or would they seize him and put him on trial on their own account? Duffy consulted various acquaintances in Durban, who advised him not to be crazy, on no account to go. But he left anyway and entered India on his British passport, no visa required. He did not raise an eyebrow at the immigration counter. He breezed through and took a taxi to Saxena's address.

Here he ran into a battery of television and print media journalists, more than 30 in all. They were fascinated to meet the man who had become legend. As with the Indian naval officers some years before, there was no antagonism at all. Saxena was charming, hospitality itself. But how long would it be before the Indian police and security establishment tumbled to it who was in their midst?

This being his first (and only) visit to India, Duffy had booked to fly to Delhi to look around before flying out. He felt a little queasy when he opened a newspaper in flight and saw his story and photograph splashed in its pages. He landed in Delhi with some apprehension, expecting the heavy hand on shoulder any moment.

But nothing happened. He saw the sights of Delhi. He visited and photographed the Taj Mahal. Then that evening he took a flight out and before too long was on a flight back to Durban.

What had the panic been? As far as he knows, Saxena himself never was reproached by the Indian authorities for having invited and harboured him. Perhaps the Indians have an extraordinary magnanimity.

***

The extraordinary thing about the Seychelles escapade is the low number of casualties occasioned. Fifty-odd mercenaries were trapped, fighting for their lives, in the airport at Mahe, surrounded, heavily outnumbered and with two clips of ammunition each. Yet the only one to die was Johan Fritz, killed by a bullet from his own side. A Tanzanian soldier was killed as he emerged from the blazing armoured car; it is not known what other Tanzanian casualties there might have been in the fighting at the barracks gates.

The Air India landing could have resulted in calamity. The aircraft could have been shot down by the Tanzanians as it approached. It could have cartwheeled in a fireball when it clipped the truck parked on the runway. Hundreds would have died, all innocent civilians. It could also have been shot down as it took off again, had the Tanzanians not observed the cease-fire. The survival of the Boeing and its passengers seems providential.

Four members of the advance party were captured after the airport debacle. Barney Carey and Aubrey Brooks were in hospital, badly beaten, when Carey, who was fluent in Swahili, heard their Tanzanian guards plotting to shoot them, right there in the ward, and claim they were trying to escape. It was only the intervention of a very brave Seychellois doctor that saved their lives.

Carey, Brooks, Roger England and Jerry Puren were subsequently put on trial for their part in the coup attempt and sentenced to death. They were later pardoned and released, Anglican Archbishop Desmond Tutu instrumental in achieving this.

Given their objectives and what they actually did – entering the country armed and not hesitating to shoot – it is as if this motley of soldiers of fortune had a guardian angel over them.

***

Duffy still lives in Durban, but now in an eccentric, low-key, almost reclusive existence. He eventually retired from the Sunday Tribune and the other newspapers in the stable. He still maintains contact with Colonel Hoare, now in his late nineties, though the ranks of the old comrades are thinning. Duffy is a raconteur of note, with remarkable clarity of recall. His stories are notable for their vividness and factual consistency. He has truly lived life. This account attempts to set it all down for the enjoyment of a wider world.

Made in the USA
San Bernardino, CA
14 November 2018